SOJOURNER'S DEVO

Sojourner's Devo

Published by C.M.H. Koenig Books LLC
www.cmhkoenigbooks.net

Sojourner's Devo: A 90-Day Devotional for the Christian Walk of Faith

The original works of Matthew Henry (1662-1714), Robert Hawker (1753-1827), Octavius Winslow (1808-1878), and Charles H. Spurgeon (1834-1892) are in the public domain.

ISBN: 978-1-956475-98-2 (Paperback)
ISBN: 978-1-956475-99-9 (eBook)

Compiled by: H.L. Rautio
Edited, with updated English, by: T.C. Milton
Cover design by: H.L. Rautio
Cover photograph by: D. Shahvaran

First Printing, 2025
Second Printing, 2026

Contents

"Once you were not a people, but now you are God's people; once you had not received mercy, but now you have received mercy.

Beloved, I urge you as sojourners and exiles to ... keep your conduct among the Gentiles honorable, so that when they speak against you as evildoers, they may see your good deeds and glorify God on the day of visitation."

(1 Peter 2:9-12, ESV)

1

Psalm 104

My soul! Read and pause over again and again this lovely hymn until your heart and every devout affection goes forth in praises to Jehovah—Father, Son, and Holy Spirit—for all the blessings here ascribed to Him, who is indeed very great, and glorious, and clothed with honor and majesty. Behold Him going forth in acts of creation, providence, goodness, and mercy! See the Lord as raising up this magnificent universe and filling it with inhabitants, not to make Himself more glorious (for that is impossible) but to make innumerable beings happy; not that He might receive but that He might impart and pour out emanations of Himself to communicate life and comfort to myriads. Hail, our glorious, great, and bountiful Jehovah!

And my soul, when you have duly pondered this wonderful subject and bent the knee in praise and humility before a God of such infinite power and majesty, as He has manifested in the outer works of nature and providence, look up for His leadings, to take you by the hand and bring you into His inner courts of grace. There let your mind be overwhelmed in contemplating a God in Christ, displaying redemption to a lost world in the person, and by the offices, of Jesus. Oh, "thou brightness of the Father's glory, and the express image of his person!" (Heb. 1:3). In the glories of Your redemption, You have gone forth for Your people, making Your angels spirits and Your ministers a flaming fire (v. 7). You send forth the springs of Your grace into the humble heart, and You water the souls of Your redeemed from above. All, all live upon You, and in You, and from Your rich communications. Help me then, Lord, to praise You, to love You, to delight in You. And let my meditation of You be sweet. Sweet it always must be, most blessed Jesus, for Your very name is as ointment poured forth. And while sinners that despise You and will not accept Your salvation shall be no more, let my unceasing song of love and praise come up before You from day to day, till I join the redeemed in their hallelujahs before Your throne forever. Amen. (Robert Hawker, Poor Man's Old Testament Commentary, vol. 4, p. 502)

2

Isaiah 55:6–9

M y soul! Have you ever considered the blessedness in this verse (v. 8), as it concerns the great work of salvation? Ponder over it this evening. There is nothing, perhaps, in which there is a greater and more striking difference than there is between our crude and limited notions of redemption and the perfect and unerring thoughts of Jehovah on this point. Our conduct with each other is so limited on the score of pardon that, though we forgive a first or second offence, if it is repeated beyond that, nature revolts at the offender and seems to find justification in withholding any further acts of mercy. Hence, we form the same standard of judgment concerning God. But with God, abounding sin calls forth abounding grace (Matt. 18:21–22) and, like the tide, rises above the high-water mark, even overflowing all the banks and surrounding ground—so much so, indeed, that it covers the mountains, and "if the sin of Judah be looked for, it shall not be found" (Jer. 50:20). Hence the prophet, in a transport of holy joy and triumph in the contemplation, cries out, "Who is a God like unto thee, that pardoneth iniquity, and passeth by the transgression of the remnant of his heritage? He retaineth not his anger forever, because he delighteth in mercy. He will turn again; he will have compassion upon us: he will subdue our iniquities! and thou wilt cast all our sins into the depths of the sea" (Mic. 7:18–19). How truly blessed, then, must it be to carry the same kind of reasoning concerning God into all our thinking in relation to Him and His dealings with us. As highly as I may be able to think concerning Him, I must fall infinitely short of what He really is, both in the nature of His existence and in all His dealings with His creatures. In those points where He has been pleased to reveal Himself, I cannot err. But if I attempt to go farther, the bar to inquiry stops my way, and this sweet verse stands for a memorandum to inform me. "For my thoughts are not your thoughts, neither are your ways my ways, saith the Lord" (Isaiah 55:8). Now grace rejoices in this discovery, while proud, unhumbled nature revolts at it. Say, my soul, do you feel delight in such views of Jehovah? Is it blessed to you that, in all your Jesus has taught you, He has brought you to see more and more of your nothingness, your littleness, and the Lord's all-sufficiency? Surely it must be divine teaching alone that can create joy in the heart, when such discoveries are made which tend to humble the creature and exalt the Creator. Blessed be the Lord, who teaches me to profit! (Hawker, The Poor Man's Evening Portion, November 3)

3

Psalm 119:97–104

Reader, let us listen to these sweet words as the words of Jesus. Let us beg of God the Holy Spirit to give us grace to feel and know our interest in what He here says, because of our interest in Him. And let us look up to God our Father, while we hear Jesus thus expressing, in our nature, His love for the law of the Father, His regard for all His commandments, and His uniform, undeviating integrity in all He came to perform. Let us plead in His name and righteousness for every covenant blessing which becomes the right of His redeemed by virtue of divine promises in the salvation by Jesus. Yes, blessed Lamb of God (John 1:29; Rev. 7:17)! Your Father's law was the whole of Your delight by day (John 4:34), and the heavenly bodies in their traveling circuit witnessed Your meditation by night. All that were before you were servants only, ministering to Your word. Prophets and patriarchs knew nothing compared to Your knowledge, the wonderful Counselor of Your people (Isa. 9:6). Let me taste of Your grace and love (Ps. 34:8), divine almighty Teacher, and may the meditation of my heart be so sweetly engaged on You that my lips may drop as the honeycomb and the name of Jesus be the first and last in my mouth all day. (Hawker, Poor Man's Old Testament Commentary, vol. 4, p. 565)

4

Colossians 1:9–12

The glorified saints are "the saints in light" (v. 12). No more veiling of the Father's countenance, no more "walking in darkness, having no light" (Isa. 50:10), no more mourning over divine desertions or suspensions of the Father's experienced love, no more tears to dim the eye, no more clouds of unbelief to darken the mind, no more mental despondency to enshroud the spirit. These glorified saints leave the gloom, and the mist, and the fog, and the darkness of ignorance, error, and pollution behind them, and they flee to the regions of light, to "the inheritance of the saints" of which "the Lamb is the light thereof" (Rev. 21:23).

But it will be observed that these glorified saints are said to be "partakers of the inheritance" (v. 12). There is something very emphatic in the word "partakers." We are partakers of it now, in Christ our Head. Because of our union to Christ, the exalted head of the church, we are at present partakers of this inheritance. We have the first realizations of it in our soul: the foretaste and, what is best of all, the indwelling of the Spirit, who is the pledge of its possession. And if we have the pledge of the inheritance in the possession of the Spirit, we must, and shall assuredly, have the inheritance itself.

"Partakers of the inheritance of the saints in light." We are partakers with all the saints of God; partakers with the whole family of the elect; partakers with all the children of adoption; partakers with Abraham, Isaac, and Jacob, with David and Solomon, and with all who have gone before us, with all who have entered heaven a little in advance; and partakers with all the "ransomed of the Lord," who shall yet "come to Zion with songs, and everlasting joy upon their heads, obtaining joy and gladness, their sorrow and their sighing fleeing away!" (Isa. 35:10). Oh, who would not be a "partaker of the inheritance of the saints in light"? Reader, if you are a humble possessor of the inner life, you shall be a happy partaker of this glorious inheritance—the life which is to come. (Octavius Winslow, Morning Thoughts, January 20)

5

Romans 13:8–12

Surely the good order of society and the general peace of states and kingdoms are promoted by wise laws and regulations, and happy is the nation who has the Lord for their God (Ps. 33:12).

But my soul, as you are looking for a city which has foundation, whose builder and maker is God, be on the watch for the Lord's coming. And be aware that to you the night of this wilderness state is far gone, and the day of the immortal world is at hand, which like the tide of a vast ocean is hastening to cover over the whole earth. Oh, for grace to be weaned from all things here below, and to be ready at a moment's warning to mount up and meet the Lord in the air. Blessed Lord Jesus, let it be my happiness to be found waiting! And may God the Spirit put Christ and His righteousness on my soul, that when my Lord shall come, I may have confidence and not be ashamed before Him at His coming. (Hawker, Poor Man's New Testament Commentary, vol. 2, pp. 342–343)

6

Luke 18:9–14

Here is another beautiful parable of our Lord's, and the occasion for which He spoke it is declared. I do not think it necessary to enlarge upon the various features of it. Every circumstance in both of the characters which Christ has drawn is descriptive of the different grounds for which they were seeking acceptance with God. And it should be observed, in order to give weight to the design of our Lord's teaching, that the Pharisee and the publican are as much living characters now as in the days of our Lord. Every man is a Pharisee who is seeking acceptance with God, either wholly or in part, by priding himself on his own good deeds, and prayers, and sacraments, and almsgiving. His only means of seeking the will of Christ is to make up his own deficiency (if there should be any). And every man may be called a publican, in the sense of this parable, who from the teaching of God the Spirit has been led to behold the sinful nature in which he was born, and the condemnation in which he is involved, both by original and by actual transgression, and is led by the Holy Spirit to God in Christ, acknowledging himself as unworthy of forgiveness, while he nonetheless seeks it in sorrow and contrition. Justification is of God in Christ. And therefore, the self-condemned, and not the self-righteous, finds justification before God. (Hawker, Poor Man's New Testament Commentary, vol. 1, pp. 465–466)

7

2 Corinthians 5:11–20

A believer's experience of the truth of God is no mere fancy. No matter how severely the experience of godliness may have been stigmatized by an unrenewed world as the offspring of a morbid imagination or the product of a fanatical mind, "he that believes in the Son of God has the witness in himself" (1 John 5:10) that he has not yielded the consent of his judgment and his affections to some "cunningly devised fable." A sense of sin, brokenness and contrition before God, faith in the atoning blood of Christ, and a sweet consciousness of pardon, acceptance, adoption, and joy in the Holy Spirit are no mere hallucinations of a disordered mind. To read one's pardon fully and fairly written out; to look up to God as one accepted and adopted; to feel the spirit going out to Him in filial love and confidence, breathing its tender and endearing epithet, "Abba, Father" (Rom. 8:15); to refer every trial, cross, and dispensation of His providence to His tender and unchangeable love; to have one's will, naturally so rebellious and perverse, completely absorbed in His; to be as a weaned child, simply and unreservedly yielded up to His disposal; and to live with patient waiting for the glory that is to be revealed—oh, this is reality, sweet, blessed, solemn reality! Holy and happy is that man whose heart is not a stranger to these truths. (Winslow, Morning Thoughts, May 27)

8

Exodus 36:1

The workmen began work without delay. When God had qualified them for the work, they applied themselves to it. Note, the talents we are entrusted with must not be laid up but laid out, not hidden in a napkin but traded with. What do we have all our gifts for but to do good with them? The artisans began when Moses called them. Even those whom God has qualified for and inclined to the service of the tabernacle must wait for a regular call to it, either extraordinary (as that of prophets and apostles) or ordinary (as that of pastors and teachers). And observe who they were that Moses called: those in whose heart God had put wisdom for this purpose, beyond their natural capacity, and whose heart stirred them up to come to the work in good faith. Note, those are to be called to the building of the gospel tabernacle whom God has by His grace made in some measure fit for the work and free to engage in it. Ability and willingness (with resolution) are the two things to be regarded in the call of ministers. Has God given them not only knowledge but also wisdom? (For those that would win souls must be wise and have their hearts stirred up to come to the work—and not for the honor only but to do it, not merely talking of it.) Then, let them come to it with full purpose of heart to go through with it. The materials which the people had contributed were delivered by Moses to the workmen. They could not create a tabernacle out of nothing, nor could they work unless they had something to work upon. The people therefore brought the materials and Moses put them into the hands of the workers. Precious souls are the materials of the gospel tabernacle; they are "built up a spiritual house" (1 Peter 2:4–5). To this end, they are to offer themselves as a free-will offering to the Lord for His service (Rom. 15:16), and they are then committed to the care of His ministers as builders, to be framed and wrought upon by their edification and increase in holiness, till they all come, like the curtains of the tabernacle, "in the unity of the faith," to be a holy temple (Eph. 2:21–22; 4:12–13). (Matthew Henry, Matthew Henry's Commentary on the Whole Bible, p. 148)

9

Hebrews 10:12-18

Here is another view of Jesus to keep alive the blessed fragrancy and, under the Spirit's influence, preserve it through the night, to the morning, and for every night and every morning that follows, until the night of death be passed and that everlasting morning breaks in upon you, in which your sun shall no more go down and Jesus Himself is your everlasting light, and your God is your glory. Look, my soul, at your Jesus as this sweet scripture sets Him forth, and behold Him in His high priestly office, at once the sacrifice, the sacrificer, and the altar on which He has offered up that one offering by which He has perfected forever them that are sanctified. And mark both the preciousness of your Jesus and the preciousness of His work. It is only one offering, and that one only offered once. For, from its eternal value and efficacy, an everlasting perfection is given to all them that are sanctified and set apart for Him. "For Christ (as the apostle in his delightful manner expresses it) being raised from the dead, dieth no more: death hath no more dominion over him. For in that he died, he died unto sin once: but in that he liveth, he liveth unto God" (Rom. 6:9–10). And what abundant precious things are contained in this view of the one offering of the Lord Jesus which the Holy Spirit is continually holding forth to the church! It is blessed to behold them, blessed to believe them, and doubly blessed to be living in the constant enjoyment of them. So vast and comprehensive is this one offering of Jesus that it has not merely procured the hopes of pardon but the certainty of it; not only brought poor sinners into a capability of being saved but absolutely saved them; and not only saved them but qualified them for happiness. Indeed, it has perfected, and that forever, them that are sanctified. And who are they? Surely all are sanctified who were set apart from everlasting, in the counsel of peace, between the persons of the Godhead, and given unto the Son in an everlasting covenant that cannot be broken. For that is the intention of those blessed words of Jesus Himself in His prayer to His Father. "That I should give eternal life to as many as thou hast given me" (John 17:1–2). And, my soul, take one observation more from this sweet scripture: this perfection, given to His people by His one offering, is forever. He has perfected forever them that are sanctified, so that the blessing runs through all eternity. The efficacy of Jesus's blood and righteousness is eternally the same. In fact, it flows as fresh, and pure, and sovereign in its pleadings now as it ever has. Hallelujah! Fold up, my soul, this blessed verse in your bosom and carry it about with you in your heart. Let it be among the first and last of your thoughts when you lie down and when you rise up. Jesus will own it and prove it to the full when you bring it before His throne. (Hawker, The Poor Man's Evening Portion, March 1)

10

Romans 15:13

I admire the gracious benediction with which the apostle closes this paragraph, for the consolation of the church in all ages. And it is not only most blessedly timed, coming after what the apostle had before said of the Gentiles, but also most sweetly worded, with an eye to Christ, whose well-known character is that He is the hope of Israel and the Savior thereof (Jer. 14:8)! He is the God of hope, as if in direct opposition to those who, having no hope, are without God in the world (Eph. 2:12). And there is a very great blessedness in the prayer, or invocation, on another account also, because all three persons of the Godhead are considered in it. For, as Christ is the hope of Israel, and the Savior thereof, so God the Father has given the church everlasting consolation and a good hope through grace. And all the aboundings of hope are the immediate work and agency of God the Holy Spirit. Reader, shall not you and I put our hearty "Amen" to this sweet and affectionate prayer of the apostle and beg of God for the unceasing aboundings of all joy and peace in believing through God the Holy Spirit? (Hawker, Poor Man's New Testament Commentary, vol. 2, pp. 351–352)

11

Psalm 25

There is a beautiful order in these expressions (vv. 4–5): first to be shown, then to be taught, and then to be led in the path of grace. How blessed it is to have the Spirit to teach, the Spirit to lead, and Jesus Himself to be the way. And all this because God in Christ is every poor sinner's salvation who trusts in Him. (Hawker, Poor Man's Old Testament Commentary, vol. 4, p. 242)

12

Colossians 3:8-17

The apostle proceeds to exhort to mutual love and compassion: "Put on therefore bowels of mercy" (v. 12). We must not only put off anger and wrath, but we must put on compassion and kindness; not only cease to do evil but learn to do well; not only not do hurt to any but do what good we can to all.

The argument here used to enforce the exhortation is very affecting: "Put on, as the elect of God, holy and beloved" (v. 12). Observe a couple points: (1) Those who are holy are the elect of God, and those who are the elect of God, and holy, are beloved—they are beloved of God and ought to be so of all men. (2) Those who are the elect of God, holy and beloved, ought to conduct themselves in everything as becomes them and so as not to lose the credit of their holiness nor the comfort of their being chosen and beloved. It is appropriate that those who are holy towards God should be lowly and loving towards all men. Observe what we must put on in particular: (1) longsuffering towards those who continue to provoke us. "Charity [love] suffereth long, as well as is kind" (1 Cor. 13:4). Many can bear a short provocation but become weary of bearing when it grows long. But we must suffer long both the injuries of men and the rebukes of divine providence. If

19

God is longsuffering to us through all our provocations of Him, we should exercise longsuffering to others in similar cases. (2) mutual forbearance, in consideration of the infirmities and deficiencies under which we all labor—"forbearing one another" (v. 13). All of us have something which needs to be borne with, and this is a good reason why we should bear with others in what is disagreeable to us. We need the same good turn from others which we are bound to show them. (Henry, Matthew Henry's Commentary on the Whole Bible, p. 2335)

13

Ephesians 4:32

The apostle sweetly closes the chapter by calling upon the church to exercise the fruits of the Spirit, instead of grieving Him. And he adopts the strongest and most persuasive of all arguments for having a tender-hearted attitude among the people of God when, suggesting a model of everything that is lovely in mutual forbearance and charity, he proposes to their view the Lord Jesus. Oh, what a volume of motives arises from the person of Christ! And how strong does the appeal to God's forgiving the church for Christ's sake come home to the heart for the brethren to forgive one another? (Hawker, Poor Man's New Testament Commentary, vol. 2, p. 670)

14

Psalm 84:7

"They go from strength to strength." There are various renderings of these words, but all of them contain the idea of progress.

Our own good translation from the Authorized Version is enough for us this morning. "They go from strength to strength." That is, they grow stronger and stronger. Usually, if we are walking, we go from strength to weakness. We start fresh and in good order for our journey, but by and by the road is rough, and the sun is hot; we sit down by the wayside, and then again painfully pursue our weary way. But the Christian pilgrim, having obtained fresh supplies of grace, is as vigorous after years of toilsome travel and struggle as when he first set out. He may not be quite so elated and buoyant, nor perhaps quite so eager and hasty in his zeal as he once was, but he is much stronger in all that constitutes real power, and he travels, if more slowly, far more surely. Some gray-haired veterans have been as firm in their grasp of truth, and as zealous in diffusing it, as they were in their younger days. Alas, it must be confessed it is often otherwise, for the love of many waxes cold and iniquity abounds. But this is their own sin and not the fault of the promise which still holds good: "The youths shall faint and be weary, and the young men shall utterly fall, but they that wait upon the Lord shall renew their strength; they shall mount up with wings as eagles, they shall run and not be weary, and they shall walk and not faint" (Isa. 40:30–31). Fretful spirits sit down and trouble themselves about the future. "Alas!" say they, "we go from affliction to affliction." Very true, O you of little faith, but you go from strength to strength also. You will never find a bundle of affliction which doesn't have bound up in the midst of it sufficient grace. God will give the strength of ripe manhood with the burden allotted to full-grown shoulders. (Charles H. Spurgeon, Morning and Evening: Daily readings, Evening, December 14)

15

Matthew 9:9–13

The call of Matthew is most interesting and serves to mark the distinguishing grace of God. His name, from *mattan* (*a gift*), seems suited to one who received the free gift of the Lord. Here was no preparation, no enquiry after Christ, no waiting at ordinances—indeed, not so much as a conscious sense in the heart of Matthew, of his want of salvation. He was sitting in his gainful office of a publican, or tax-gatherer—an office odious to all the people of Israel and when exercised by a descendant of Israel, even more hateful. Such was Matthew, and so he was occupied when the Lord Jesus passed by and called him from being a tax-gatherer to become an apostle and evangelist. Oh, what grace was here! How truly was that scripture fulfilled, "I am found of them that sought me not" (Isa 65:1). What an astonishing instance of mercy was this. How very powerful must the call have been! How gracious on the part of Jesus! How surprising to the heart of Matthew! And observe the instant effects: As soon as Jesus calls, Matthew obeys. And as Jesus opened Matthew's heart to receive Him, Matthew opens his house to welcome Jesus. Neither is this all. For as this one publican had found mercy from the Lord, Matthew invited other publicans to come and find mercy also.

There is enough in Christ for all. What a lovely view to behold the Great Redeemer encircled at Matthew's table with publicans and sinners! The murmuring of the Pharisees is just as might be expected, and such as has marked Pharisees in all ages. But what a lovely answer the Lord gave to the charge. The very character of Christ, as the Physician of the soul, naturally led Him to places of sickness for the exercise of His profession. And by referring them to that memorable passage in the prophet Hosea, Jesus took the words as applicable to Himself in confirmation of His office: "Jehovah Rophe, I am the Lord that healeth thee" (Hos. 6:1; Exod. 15:26). (Hawker, Poor Man's New Testament Commentary, vol. 1, p. 63)

16

John 13:1-16

Every soul re-cast into this model, every mind conformed to this pattern, and every life reflecting this image is an exalting and a glorifying of the Son of God. There is no single practical truth in the Word of God on which the Spirit is more emphatic than the example which Christ has set for the imitation of His followers. The church needed a perfect pattern, a flawless model. It required an impersonation, a living embodiment of those precepts of the gospel so strictly enjoined upon every believer, and God has graciously set before us our true model. "Whom he did foreknow, he also did predestinate to be conformed to the image of his Son" (Rom. 8:29). And what says Christ Himself? "My sheep follow me" (John 10:27). We allow that there are points in which we cannot and are not required literally and strictly to follow Christ. We cannot lay claim to His infallibility. He who sets himself up as infallible in his judgment, spotlessly pure in his heart, and perfect in his attainments in holiness deceives his own soul. Jesus did many things, too, as our Surety, which we cannot do. We cannot drink of the cup of divine trembling which He drank, nor can we be baptized with the baptism of blood with which He was baptized. He did many things as a Jew—was circumcised, kept the

Passover—which are not obligatory upon us. And yet, in all that is essential to our sanctification, to our holy, obedient, God-glorifying walk, He has "left us an example, that we should follow his steps" (1 Peter 2:21). He left us an example in His lowly spirit, meek and humble deportment, and patient endurance of suffering: "Learn of me, for I am meek and lowly in heart" (Matt. 11:29). And He left us an example in the disinterestedness of His love, His pure benevolence, the unselfishness of His religion: "Look not every man on his own things, but every man also on the things of others: let this mind be you which was also in Christ Jesus" (Phil. 2:4–5). "For even Christ pleased not himself" (Rom. 15:2–4). Look not every man on his own circle, his own family, his own gifts, his own interests, comfort, and happiness, his own church, his own community, his own minister. Let him not look upon these exclusively. Let him not prefer his own advantage to the public good. Let him not be self-willed in matters involving the peace and comfort of others. Let him not form favorite theories or individual opinions to the hazard of a church's prosperity or of a family's happiness. Let him yield, sacrifice, and give place rather than carry a point to the detriment of others. Let him, with a generous, magnanimous, disinterested spirit in all things imitate Jesus, who "pleased not himself." Let him seek the good of others, honoring their gifts, respecting their opinions, nobly yielding when they correct and overrule his own. Let him promote the peace of the church, consult the honor of Christ, and seek the glory of God above and beyond all private and selfish ends. This is what it means to be conformed to the image of God's dear Son, to which high calling we are predestined. And in any feature of resemblance which the Holy Spirit brings out in the holy life of a follower of the Lamb, Christ is thereby glorified before men and angels. (Winslow, Morning Thoughts, September 29)

17

Romans 5:17–21

Pause, my soul, and put forth your fullest thoughts in contemplation of the two united sources of felicity marked in this verse: the Father's eternal purpose in the reign of grace and the everlasting efficacy and infinite value of Jesus's righteousness to eternal life. None but God Himself can know the fullness and extent of either. I am persuaded that angels of light can never entertain adequate conceptions of either. The eternal purpose of God has put a limit on the reign of sin—it is only unto death. But those purposes give a further extent to the redemption from death and sin by Jesus, because the glory of Christ's person and the worth of His salvation possess, in both, a vast overplus, a redundancy of merit, which brings the redeemed into favor and acceptance in Jesus. And it does this with such everlasting felicity that eternity itself can never exhaust it nor fully recompense or pay for it. Oh, for grace to contemplate the love of the Father and the Son by this standard! Lord, I would be lost; I would be swallowed up day by day in unceasing meditation. Dearest, blessed, precious Jesus! Let me think of nothing else, speak of nothing else but, by faith, possess with anticipation the joys of Your redeemed until I come, through You and in You, to the everlasting enjoyment of them in

Your kingdom of glory. (Hawker, The Poor Man's Morning Portion, January 23)

18

Hebrews 11:1

Now faith is the *substance* of things hoped for, the *evidence* of things not seen. There is something very striking in this account of faith as given by the Holy Spirit Himself. It is called by Him a substance, meaning that the object on which the soul rests is substantially formed in the mind and realized, so that the mind becomes as perfectly assured of its existence and reality as though it were seen. This is faith. And in this sense, it is the substance of things which are at a distance but are nonetheless as perfectly alive to the soul as though they were present to bodily sense. Let us explain great things by a smaller example: I have a child, a friend, or a relation whom I have never seen and who lives at a distance from me. But I am continually receiving signs from him, by message or letter, both of his existence and of his affection towards me. Now, though I have never seen him, I no more doubt his being and existence than my own. I therefore substantiate, and realize in my mind, this certainty, and I am motivated by it accordingly. Such, but in an infinitely higher degree, are the great objects of faith in relation to things supernatural and unseen. I have received evidence upon evidence and love tokens multiplied with love tokens from Jesus my Lord. By faith, therefore, I substantiate and realize all those blessed things concerning Jesus. And it is real to me. Jesus says, "I will cause them that love me to inherit substance, and I will fill their treasures" (Prov. 8:21). Hence, therefore, as the apostle says in relation to Jesus, "Whom having not seen we love; in whom though now we see him not, yet believing, we rejoice with joy unspeakable, and full of glory; receiving the end of our faith, even the salvation of our souls" (1 Peter 1:8–9). It was thus with Abraham and other holy men of old. Their faith did not need the presence of what they believed in. God's testimony concerning it was enough. It became, therefore, the substance of things hoped for, the evidence of things not seen. (Hawker, Poor Man's New Testament Commentary, vol. 3, pp. 287–288)

19

John 14:6–7

Almighty Preacher! Give me grace to sit at Your feet and hear by faith Your sweet and all-powerful voice in this unequalled sermon, causing all the gracious truths of it to sink deep in my heart. Yes, dearest Lord, You are indeed "the way, and the truth, and the life" (v. 6). None can have access to God but by You. God has set You up in Your Mediator character. And in You and by You, as the life and the light of Your people, Your whole church has access by one Spirit to the Father.

Welcome holy and eternal God the Spirit to Your church! You are indeed the very Comforter, for Your great work, Lord, is consolation. Oh, let me know You in Your sweet manifestations, in comforting my poor soul under all discouragements, with the suitableness of Christ. Yes, Lord, in all Your gifts and graces make known to me the glory, the grace, the love, the infinite tenderness and compassion of my God and Savior as You show me all these things in Christ. Let it be my unceasing happiness to be brought daily, even hourly, under Your quickening [making spiritually alive], refreshing, soul-reviving influences, that I may be filled with that "joy which is unspeakable and full of glory, receiving the end of my faith, even the salvation of my soul" (1 Peter 1:8–9).

SOJOURNER'S DEVO | 33

Father of mercies and God of all grace! Blessed, forever blessed, be that everlasting love which has followed up the manifestation of God's dear Son with the manifestation of God's Holy Spirit. Thanks be to God for His unspeakable gift! (Hawker, Poor Man's New Testament Commentary, vol. 1, p. 660)

20

Luke 8:5–18

Let us observe several things from this parable and the explanation of it. The heart of man is as soil to the seed of God's Word. It is capable of receiving it and bringing forth the fruits of it, but unless that seed is sown in it, it will bring forth nothing valuable. Our care, therefore, must be to bring the seed and the soil together. To what purpose do we have the seed in this scripture, if it is not sown? And to what purpose do we have the soil in our own hearts, if it is not sown with that seed?

It is not enough that the fruit is brought forth. It must be brought to perfection; it must be fully ripened. If it is not, it is as if there were no fruit at all brought forth, for that which in Matthew and Mark is said to be unfruitful is the same that here is said to bring forth none to perfection (v. 14). For perseverance is necessary to the perfection of a work.

The good ground, which brings forth good fruit, is an honest and good heart that is well disposed to receive instruction and commandment. A heart free from sinful pollutions and firmly fixed for God and duty—an upright heart, a tender heart, and a heart that trembles at the Word—is an honest and good heart which, having heard the Word, *understands* it (so it is in Matthew), *receives* it (so it is in Mark), and *keeps* it (so it is here), just as the soil not only receives but keeps the seed, and the stomach not only receives but keeps the food or medicine.

Where the Word is well kept there is fruit brought forth with patience (v. 15). This also is added here. There must be both *bearing* patience and *waiting* patience—patience to suffer the tribulation and persecution which may arise because of the Word and patience to continue to the end in well-doing.

In consideration of all this, we ought to take heed how we hear (v. 18.); take heed of those things that will hinder our profiting by the Word we hear, watch over our hearts in hearing, and take heed lest they betray us; take heed lest we hear carelessly and slightly, lest, upon any account, we entertain prejudice against the Word we hear; and take heed to the frame of our spirits after we have heard the Word, lest we lose what we have gained. (Henry, Matthew Henry's Commentary on the Whole Bible pp. 1848-1849)

21

Psalm 31

God is good to all, but He is, in a special manner, good to Israel (referring to ancient Israelites and believers in the New Covenant). His goodness to them is wonderful and will be, to eternity, a matter of admiration. "O how great is thy goodness" (v. 19)! How profound are the counsels of it! How rich are the treasures of it! How free and extensive are the communications of it! Those very persons whom men load with slanders God loads with benefits and honors. Those who are recipients of this goodness are described to be such as fear God and trust in Him, as stand in awe of His greatness and rely on His grace. This goodness is said to be laid up for them and made effectual for them.

There is a goodness laid up for them in the other world, an inheritance reserved in heaven (1 Peter 1:4), and there is a goodness wrought for them in this world, goodness made effectual in them. There is enough in God's goodness both for the portion and inheritance of all His children when they come to their full age and for their maintenance and education during their minority. There is enough in the bank and enough in hand.

This goodness is laid up in His promise for all that fear God, to whom assurance is given that they shall lack no good thing.

But it is made effectual, in the actual performance of the promise, for those that trust in Him—those who by faith take hold of the promise, put it into practice, and draw out to themselves the benefit and comfort of it. If what is laid up for us in the treasures of the everlasting covenant is not made effectual for us, it is our own fault, because we do not believe. But for those who trust in God, just as they have the comfort of His goodness in their own souls, so they have the benefit of it (and the benefit of an estate goes far with some); it is made effectual for them before the sons of men. God's goodness to them puts an honor upon them and rolls away their reproach, for "all that see them shall acknowledge them, that they are the seed which the Lord hath blessed" (Isa. 61:9).

God preserves man and beast, but He is, in a special manner, the protector of His own people. "Thou shalt hide them" (v. 20). As His goodness is hidden and reserved for them, so they are hidden and preserved for it. The saints are God's hidden ones. See here, first, the danger they are in, which arises from the pride of man and from the quarrel of tongues. Proud men insult them and would trample on them and tread them down; contentious men pick quarrels with them, and, when tongues are at war, good people often receive the worst. The pride of men endangers their liberty; the quarrel of tongues in perverse arguments endangers truth. But second, see the defense they are under: "Thou shalt hide them in the secret of thy presence ... in a pavilion" (v 20). God's providence shall keep them safe from the malice of their enemies. He has many ways of sheltering them. When Baruch and Jeremiah were sought out, the Lord hid them (Jer. 36:26). God's grace shall keep them safe from the evil of the judgments that are around them. To them they have no sting, and they shall be hidden in the day of the Lord's anger, for there is no anger at them. His comforts shall keep them easy and cheerful; His sanctuary, where they have

communion with Him, shelters them from the fiery darts of ter-
ror and temptation; and the mansions in His house above shall be
shortly, and eternally, their hiding place from all danger and fear.
(Henry, Matthew Henry's Commentary on the Whole Bible, pp.
784–785)

22

Proverbs 12:25

Here is, first, the cause and consequence of melancholy. It is "heaviness in the heart"; it is a load of care, and fear, and sorrow upon the spirits, depressing them and disabling them to exert themselves with any vigor on what is to be done or fortitude in what is to be borne. It makes them stoop; it prostrates and sinks them. Those that are thus oppressed can neither do the duty nor take the comfort of any relation, condition, or conversation. Those, therefore, that are inclined to it should watch and pray against it. Second, we see the cure of it: "A good word" from God, applied by faith, makes the heart glad. Once such good word ... is, "Cast thy burden upon the Lord, and he shall sustain thee" (Ps. 55:22). The good word of God, particularly the gospel, is designed to make the hearts glad that are weary and heavy laden (see also Matt. 11:28). Ministers are to be helpers of this joy. (Henry, Matthew Henry's Commentary on the Whole Bible, p. 981)

23

Romans 12:12-15

There is not only a great loveliness in the Christian graces which the apostle has enumerated in these verses, but also a beautiful order in the manner in which he has marked them down. Rejoicing in hope is very appropriately placed before being patient in tribulation. And rejoicing with the happy comes before weeping with them that weep. For until the child of God is established in the grace of hope, he cannot know how to minister consolation to others. Neither can one mingle the tear of grace with the mourner unless he himself has had his own tears mingled with the spiced wine of the pomegranate [a symbol of joy and refreshing]. I refer the reader to my commentary on these points for the right understanding, according to my view, of those sweet and gracious actions. (see also Rom. 5:1-5 and Matt. 5:1-12) (Hawker, Poor Man's New Testament Commentary, vol. 2, p. 336)

24

Philippians 2:1–11

What is it to have "the mind that was in Christ"? We answer that it is to be ever aiming after the highest perfection of holiness. It is to have the eye of faith perpetually on Jesus as our model, studying Him closely as our great example, seeking conformity to Him in all things. It is to be regulated in all our conduct by His humble spirit. First, with regard to others, to choose the low place, to acknowledge God in, and to glorify Him for, the grace, gifts, and usefulness bestowed on other saints, and to exemplify in our social communion the self-denying, expansive benevolence of the gospel. This creates the duty of not seeking first our own interests but rather of sacrificing all self-gratification, and even honor and advantage, if, by so doing, we may promote the happiness and welfare of others. Thus, it is to live not for ourselves but for God and our fellow men, for "no man lives to himself, and no man dies to himself" (Rom. 14:7). In the spirit of Him who, on the eve of returning to His glory, took a towel and girded Himself and washed His disciples' feet, it is to serve the saints in the most lowly acts and offices. Second, it is to exemplify, with regard to ourselves, the same humble spirit which He breathed. It is to be little in our own eyes, to cherish a humble estimate of our gifts, attainments, usefulness, and station, to be meek, gentle, and submissive under rebuke and correction, to "seek not great things for ourselves" (Jer. 45:5), to court not human praise, watching our hearts with perpetual vigilance and jealousy, lest we thirst for the honor which comes from man and not "the honor that comes from God only" (John 5:44). It is to contribute to the necessities of saints without begrudging, to give to Christ's cause without ostentation, to do good in secret, to seek, in all our works of zeal and benevolence and charity, to hide ourselves, that self may be perpetually mortified—in a word, it is to hunger and thirst after righteousness, to be poor in spirit and lowly in mind, to walk humbly with God, and to live to, labor for, and aim after the glory of God in all things. This is to have the "mind which was also in Christ Jesus." (Winslow, Morning Thoughts, March 8)

25

2 Corinthians 8:8–9

Reader, do not hastily leave this wonderful subject. Think of the grace of our Lord Jesus Christ. He was rich. Yes, so rich that, as God, all divine perfections were His in common with the Father and the Holy Spirit. And as God-man, in Him dwelt all the fullness of the Godhead bodily. All government was His, in His universal empire and dominion, through all the departments of nature, providence, grace, and glory. All things were made by Him and for Him. He is before all things, and by Him all things consist. All these were, and are, His by right, by possession—essentially and truly His own, underived, eternal, and unchangeable. Now behold His vast humiliation. Though He was thus rich beyond the utmost imagination of riches, yet for our sakes, He became poor. So poor that He had nowhere to lay His head. He was despised and rejected of men, a man of sorrows, as if (and which was in reality the case) no sorrow nor all the sorrows of the human state could be brought into comparison with His (Lam. 1:12). And all this, that His people through His poverty might be made rich. And what tends to enhance the mercy still more is the persons to whom this love of Christ was thus shown—not angels or holy men but sinners, and those of the deepest dye, yes, enemies of God, by wicked works, who had done nothing to merit divine favor but had rather done everything to merit divine displeasure. "Herein is love, not that we loved God, but that he loved us" (1 John 4:10)! Reader, do you know this grace of the Lord Jesus Christ? Many read of it; many talk of it. But Paul tells the church of the Corinthians that they *knew* it; that is, God the Holy Spirit had taught them to know it, in the blessed effect of it upon their souls, by regeneration. By this they knew the truth of it and of their interest in it. For having been once desperately poor and ruined by sin, they knew themselves now immensely rich in Christ. Does my reader know it, and from the same cause? (Hawker, Poor Man's New Testament Commentary, vol. 2, pp. 535–536)

26

Psalm 42:8–11

Songs in the night! Who can create them? Midnight harmony! Who can inspire it? God can, and God does. The "God of all consolation" (Rom. 15:4–6), the "God who comforts those who are cast down" (2 Cor. 7:6), the "God of hope" (Rom. 15:13), who causes the "bright and morning star" (Rev. 22:16) to rise upon the dreary landscape, the "God of peace, who Himself gives peace, always and by all means" (2 Thess. 3:16)—even He, our Maker and Redeemer, gives songs in the night. Music, at all times sweet, is the sweetest amid the sublimity of night. When in the solemn stillness that reigns (not a breath rustling the leaves, and Echo [the ever-talkative Greek nymph] herself slumbering), when in the darkness that enshrouds, the thoughts that agitate, the gloomy phantoms that flit before the imagination like shadows dancing upon the wall, there breaks upon the wakeful ear the soft notes of skillfully touched instruments, blending with the melting tones of well-tuned voices, it is as though angels had come down to serenade and soothe the sad and jaded sons of earth. But there are songs richer, and there is music sweeter still than theirs: the songs which God gives and the music which Jesus inspires in the long dark night of the Christian's pilgrimage. A saint of God is then a happy man. He is often most so when others deem him most miserable. When they, gazing with pity upon his adversities and his burdens and silently marking the conflict of thought and feeling passing within (compared with which external trial is but as the bubble floating upon the surface), deem him a fit object of their commiseration and sympathy, even then there is a hidden spring of joy, an undercurrent of peace, lying in the depths of the soul which renders him, chastened and afflicted though he is, a happy and an enviable man. "Blessed are those who mourn now, for they shall be comforted" (Matt. 5:4). (Winslow, Evening Thoughts, January 2)

27

John 17:17–19

Sanctification begins in regeneration. The Spirit of God infuses into man that new living principle by which he becomes "a new creature" in Christ Jesus. This work, which begins in the new birth, is carried on in two ways—mortification, whereby the lusts of the flesh are subdued and kept under, and vivification, by which the life which God has put within us is made to be a well of water springing up unto everlasting life. This is carried on every day in what is called "perseverance," by which the Christian is preserved and continued in a gracious state and is made to abound in good works unto the praise and glory of God. The work culminates, or comes to perfection, in "glory," when the soul, being thoroughly purged, is caught up to dwell with holy beings at the right hand of the Majesty on High. But while the Spirit of God is thus the author of sanctification, there is a visible agency employed which must not be forgotten. "Sanctify them," said Jesus, "through thy truth: thy word is truth" (v. 17). The passages of Scripture which prove that the instrument of our sanctification is the Word of God are very many. The Spirit of God brings to our minds the precepts and doctrines of truth and applies them with power. These are heard in the ear, and being received in the heart, they work in us to will and to do of God's good pleasure. The truth is the sanctifier, and if we do not hear or read the truth, we shall not grow in sanctification. We only progress in sound living as we progress in sound understanding. "Thy word is a lamp unto my feet and a light unto my path" (Ps. 119:105). Do not say of any error, "It is a mere matter of opinion." No man indulges an error of judgment without sooner or later tolerating an error in practice. Hold fast the truth, for by so holding the truth shall you be sanctified by the Spirit of God. (Spurgeon, Morning and Evening: Daily readings, Morning, July 4)

28

1 Timothy 1:15-17

Let the reader note the view Paul had of the divine mercy shown to him in putting him into the ministry—one who was previously a blasphemer, a persecutor, and an injurious threat to the church. He evidently alludes here to the awful conduct he was pursuing at the time of his conversion. Paul seems to imply that, just as there is a fullness of the iniquity of the Amorite before which point there is no ripeness for destruction (Gen. 15:16), so there is a fullness of transgression which the Lord's chosen ones heap up in the Adam-nature of their fallen state before the time of their conversion arrives, so that the recovery from it tends to heighten to their astonished view, as they look back upon the past, the Lord's long-suffering and their heights of daring rebellion. In the instance of Paul, he called to mind how he had, by his cruelties, compelled the saints of God to blaspheme. This seems to have wrought upon his mind, in the recollection of it, the bitterest part of his desperately wicked provocations. Reader, observe to what length God's chosen ones run in offenses! And observe in the midst of all, when sinning with a high hand, how the Lord still is watching over them and, in spite of all hell's temptations, keeping them from the unpardonable sin! Oh, the wonders of grace! What a subject this will be, to be opened in every child of God when we come into eternity! (Hawker, Poor Man's New Testament Commentary, vol 3, p. 128)

29

Acts 28:1-2

Notice the kind reception which the inhabitants of this island gave to the distressed strangers that were shipwrecked on their coast: "The barbarous people showed us no little kindness." God had promised that there should be no loss of any man's life, and, "as for God, his work is perfect" (Ps. 18: 30). If they had escaped the sea and when they came ashore had perished for cold or want, the outcome would have been the same. Therefore, Providence continues its care of them, and what benefits we receive by the hand of man must be acknowledged to come from the hand of God. For every creature is to us what He makes them to be, and no more. And when He pleases, just as He can make enemies to be at peace, so He can make strangers to be friends—friends in need—and those are friends indeed, friends in adversity, and that is the time that a brother is born for.

Observe the general notice taken of the kindness which the natives of Malta showed to Paul and his company. They are called barbarous people because they did not, in language and customs, conform either to the Greeks or Romans, who looked (condescendingly enough) upon everyone but themselves as barbarians, though otherwise civilized enough and perhaps in some cases more civil than they. These so-called barbarous people, however, were full of humanity: "They showed us no little kindness." So far were they from making a prey of this shipwreck (as many, I fear, who are called Christian people would have done) that they laid hold of it as an opportunity of showing mercy. The Samaritan is a better neighbor to the poor wounded man than the priest or Levite. And truly we have not found greater humanity among Greeks, or Romans, or Christians than among these barbarous people. And it is written for our imitation, that we may hence learn to be compassionate to those that are in distress and misery and to relieve and help them to the utmost of our ability, as those that know we ourselves are also in the body. We should be ready to entertain strangers, as Abraham, who sat at his tent door to invite strangers in (Heb. 13:2), but especially strangers in distress, as these were. "Honor all men" (1 Peter 2:17). If Providence has so appointed the bounds of our habitation as to give us an opportunity of being frequently helpful to persons at a loss, we should not place it among the inconveniences of our lot but the advantages of it, because "it is more blessed to give than to receive" (Acts 20:35). Who knows but that these barbarous people had their lot cast in this island for such a time as this!

We read in our passage of a particular instance of their kindness: "They kindled a fire" in some large hall or other, and they "received us everyone"; that is, they made room for us around the fire and welcomed all of us to it, without asking either what country we were from or what religion we followed. In swimming to the shore and clinging to the broken pieces of the ship, we must suppose that they were sadly wet, that they didn't have a dry thread on them. And, as if that were not enough, to complete the deluge, waters from above met those from below, and it rained so hard that this would quickly wet them to the skin. And it was a cold rain, too, so that they wanted nothing so much as a good fire (for they had eaten heartily just before on board the ship), and this they got for them presently, to warm them and dry their clothes. It is sometimes as much charity to poor families to supply them with fuel as with food or raiment. "Be you warmed" is as necessary as "Be you filled." When, in the circumstances of bad weather, we find ourselves protected from the rigors of the season by the accommodations of a warm house, bed, clothes, and a good fire, we should think how many lie exposed to the present rain and cold, and we should pity them, and pray for them, and help them if we can.

When the fire was to be made, and made bigger, that so great a company might all have the benefit of it, Paul was as busy as any of them in gathering sticks. Though he was free from all, and of greater importance than any of them, he made himself servant of all. Paul was an industrious, active man and loved to be doing whatever needed to be done, never seeking to take his ease. Paul was a humble, self-denying man, and he would stoop to anything by which he might be of service, even to the gathering of sticks to make a fire. We should consider nothing as beneath us except for sin, and we should be willing to condescend to the most humble work, if there is occasion, for the good of our brethren. The people are ready to help them, yet Paul, wet and cold as he is, will not put it all upon them but will help himself. Those that receive benefit by the fire should help to carry fuel to it. (Henry, Matthew Henry's Commentary on the Whole Bible, pp. 2187–2188)

30

Romans 1:8-12

I would request the reader to notice here what Paul expected from seeing the Christians in Rome; namely, that while through grace he might be enabled to impart to them some spiritual gift, he himself, though so great an apostle, might receive from them comfort. It is devoutly to be wished that this statement of Paul's were more generally regarded in our churches, both by ministers and people. The apostle here speaks of a mutual faith. And surely, as the faith is the same in all the members of Christ's body in all its properties, all flowing from one and the same fountain, which is Christ, no matter how different the greatness or smallness of the stream, it must be, or ought to be, a faith which works by love. And therefore, the consequences would be truly blessed if they were thus sought for. And it is very blessed both to the minister and his people when the people are refreshed in the Lord from the labors of His servant and the minister is comforted in his people's (and his own) growth in grace by the Word. Paul felt the sweetness of this, and so must all faithful ministers when they can adopt Paul's language. He told the Corinthians that they had acknowledged his labors in part, and he said to them, "We are your rejoicing, even as ye also are ours, in the day of the Lord Jesus" (2 Cor. 1:11–14). (Hawker, Poor Man's New Testament Commentary, vol. 2, pp. 241–242)

31

Luke 15:4–5

Here is the gentleness of the shepherd: "He lays it on his shoulders" (v. 5). Too feeble itself to walk, too exhausted in its wanderings to return, the gentle shepherd, having sought and found it, "lays it on his shoulders, rejoicing." Touching picture of the Savior's gentleness in restoring a backsliding soul! What else but infinite gentleness is seen in the restoring of Peter? It was but a look—not a word fell from the lips of the Savior; not an unkind rebuke, not a harsh upbraiding word did He breathe. Yet that look, so full of love, so full of gentleness, so full of forgiveness, did seem to say, "I am going to die for you, Peter. All this and more I suffer for you. Will you, can you, deny Me?" That look—so touching, so melting, so eloquent, and so forgiving—reached the heart of the backsliding apostle, melted it, broke it, and sent him from the judgment hall weeping bitterly. There was no expression in the look which Jesus bent upon Peter but love. Let this truth be fixed in the heart of every backsliding believer: the Lord restores the soul gently. The moment He reveals to the soul its sin, He conveys some token of His pardoning mercy. The balm is applied the moment the wound is given; the remedy is at hand the moment the disease is discovered. There is a tenderness, an unutterable tenderness, in the heart and hand, in the mercy and the method of the Lord's recovery of His child, which only He can feel.

See it in the case of David. How did God bring his sin to remembrance? By the chastising rod? By heavy judgment? By severe expressions of displeasure? No, none of these were His messengers. But He sent a kind, tender, faithful prophet to show him his awful backsliding. And the astounding words "You are the man" had scarcely died away upon his ear before he pours in this healing balm: "The Lord also has put away your sin; you shall not die" (2 Sam. 12:7–13). Oh, what gentleness, what tenderness, are thus shown in the Lord's restoring of His wandering child! From whom could this have been expected but from Him whose nature and name are love? From whom, but Him who could speak to His backsliding Ephraim, "Is Ephraim my dear son? Is he a pleasant child? For since I spoke against him, I do earnestly remember him still; therefore, my affections are troubled for him: I will surely have mercy upon him, says the Lord" (Jer. 31:20). This is an outgushing of tenderness towards a poor, returning, backsliding soul which could only have had its dwelling place in the heart of Jehovah. All real return of a backsliding soul is through Jesus. Jesus is God's great door of approach to His throne. No other entrance will conduct us to the golden scepter; no other will bring us to the Holy of Holies. Thus has the Holy Spirit unfolded this truth: "Having therefore, brethren, boldness to enter into the holiest by the blood of Jesus, by a new and living way, which he has consecrated for us, through the veil, that is to say, his flesh; and having an high priest over the house of God; let us draw near." (Heb. 10:19–22) Oh, blessed door of return for a poor, backsliding, heart-broken believer—a crucified Savior, in whom God is well pleased and for whose sake He can receive the sinner and put away his sin and can welcome the backslider and heal his backsliding! (Winslow, Evening Thoughts, August 31)

32

Matthew 10:40–42

Christ so heartily espouses His children's cause as to show Himself a friend to all their friends and to repay all the kindnesses that should at any time be bestowed upon them. "He that receiveth you, receiveth me" (v. 40).

Jesus Christ considers what is done to His faithful ministers, whether in kindness or in unkindness, as having been done to Himself and reckons Himself treated as they are treated. "He that receiveth you, receiveth me." Honor or contempt put upon an ambassador reflects honor or contempt upon the prince that sends him, and ministers are "ambassadors for Christ" (2 Cor. 5:20). See how Christ may still be honored by those who would profess their respects to Him. We always have His people and ministers with us, and He is with them always, even to the end of the world. Indeed, the honor rises higher: "He that receiveth me, receiveth him that sent me." Not only does Christ take it as having been done to Himself, but through Christ, God does too. By entertaining Christ's ministers, they entertain not only angels unawares (Heb. 13:2) but also Christ, yes, and God Himself. "When saw we thee an hungered?" (Matt. 25:37).

Kindnesses shown to Christ's people and ministers shall not only be accepted but richly and suitably rewarded. There is a great deal to be gotten by doing good service to Christ's disciples. If it be done to the Lord, He will repay them again, with interest, for He is "not unrighteous to forget any labor of love" (Heb. 6:10).

They shall receive a reward (v. 41) and in no way lose it. He does not say that they deserve a reward; we cannot merit anything as wages from the hand of God. But they shall receive a reward from the free gift of God, and they shall in no way lose it, as often happens among men because they who should reward them are either false or forgetful. The reward may be deferred—the full reward will be deferred till the resurrection of the just—but it shall in no way be lost nor shall they be losers in any way by the delay. (Henry, Matthew Henry's Commentary on the Whole Bible, pp. 1664–1665)

33

Romans 3:21-26

By a change of place with the church, Christ becomes the "Lord our Righteousness," and we are "made the righteousness of God in Him" (2 Cor. 5:20–21). There is the transfer of sin to the innocent, and, in return, there is the transfer of righteousness to the guilty. In this method of justification, no violence whatsoever is done to the moral government of God. So far from a shade obscuring its glory, that glory beams forth with a radiance which would have remained forever veiled except for the redemption of man by Christ. God never appears so like Himself as when He sits in judgment upon a sinner and determines his standing before Him upon the ground of that satisfaction to His law rendered by the Son of God in the place of the guilty. Then does He appear infinitely holy yet infinitely gracious, infinitely just yet infinitely merciful. Love, as if it had long been longing for an outlet, now leaps forth and embraces the sinner while justice, holiness, and truth gaze upon the wondrous spectacle with infinite satisfaction and delight. And shall we not pause for admiration and gratitude for Him who was constrained to stand in our place of degradation and woe that we might stand in His place of righteousness and glory? What wondrous love! What stupendous grace, that He should have been willing to take upon Himself our sin, and curse, and woe! The exchange to Him—how humiliating! He could only raise us by Himself stooping. He could only emancipate us by wearing our chain. He could only deliver us from death by Himself dying. He could only invest us with the spotless robe of His pure righteousness by wrapping around Himself the leprous mantle of our sin and curse. Oh, how precious ought He to be to every believing heart! What affection, what service, what sacrifice, what devotion He deserves at our hands! Lord, incline my heart to yield itself supremely to You! But in what way does this great blessing of justification become ours? In other words, what is the instrument by which the sinner is justified? The answer is at hand in the text "through faith in His blood" (v. 25). Faith, and faith alone, makes this righteousness of God ours. "By Him all that believe are justified" (Acts 13:39). And why is it solely and exclusively by faith? The answer is at hand: "Therefore it is of faith, that it might be by grace" (Rom. 4:16). Were justification through any other medium than by believing, the perfect freeness of the blessing would not be secured. The expression is "justified freely by His grace"; that is, gratuitously, absolutely for nothing. Not only was God in no sense whatever bound to justify the sinner, but the sovereignty of His law, as well as the sovereignty of His love, demanded that, in extending to the sinner the greatest boon of His government, He should do so upon no other principle than as a perfect act of grace on the part of the Giver and as a perfect gratuity on the part of the recipient, having "nothing to pay." Therefore, whatever is joined with faith in the matter of the sinner's justification—whether it be baptism, or any other rite, or any work or condition performed by the creature—renders the act entirely void and of no effect. The justification of the believing sinner is as free as the God of love and grace can make it. (Winslow, Morning Thoughts, December 17)

34

Matthew 8:18–27

C hrist had given sailing orders to His disciples, that they should depart to the other side of the sea of Tiberias, into the country of Gadara, in the tribe of Gad, which lay east of Jordan. There He would go to rescue a poor creature that was possessed with a legion of devils, though He foresaw how He should be insulted there.

Now, He chose to go by water. It would not have made much difference if He had gone by land, but He chose to cross the lake so that He might have an opportunity to manifest Himself as the God of the sea as well as of the dry land and to show that all power was His, both in heaven and in earth (Matt. 28:18). It is a comfort to those who go down to the sea in ships, and are often in perils there, to reflect that they have a Savior to trust in and pray to who knows what it is to be at sea and to be in storms there. But observe, when He went to sea, He had no yacht or pleasure-boat to attend Him but made use of His disciples' fishing boats, so poorly was He accommodated in all respects.

"His disciples followed him" (v. 23). The twelve kept close to Him when others stayed behind upon the *terra firma*, where there was sure footing. Note that they, and they only, will be found the true disciples of Christ who are willing to go to sea with Him, to follow Him into dangers and difficulties. Many would be content to go the land way to heaven who would rather stand still, or go back, than venture upon a dangerous sea. But those who would rest with Christ hereafter must follow Him now, wherever He leads them—into a ship or into a prison, as well as into a palace. (Henry, Matthew Henry's Commentary on the Whole Bible, p. 1651)

35

Psalm 86:8–13

This psalm is entitled "A Prayer of David." Probably it was not penned upon any particular occasion but was a prayer he often used himself and recommended to others for their use, especially in a day of affliction. Many think that David penned this prayer as a type of Christ, "who in the days of his flesh offered up strong cries" (Heb. 5:7). David, in this prayer (according to the nature of that duty), gives glory to God. He seeks for grace and favor from God, that God would hear his prayers, preserve and save him, and be merciful to him, that He would give him joy, and grace, and strength and put honor upon him. He pleads God's goodness and the malice of his enemies. In singing this, we must, as David did, lift up our souls to God in petition.

For the operations of God's grace in him, he prays that God would give him an understanding heart, that He would inform and instruct him concerning his duty. "Teach me thy way, O Lord!" (v. 11), the way that You have appointed me to walk in. When I am in doubt concerning it, make it plain to me what I should do; let me hear Your voice saying, "This is the way" (Isa. 30:21). David was well taught in the things of God, and yet he knew he needed further instruction and many times could not trust his own judgment. "Teach me thy way; I will walk in thy truth" (Ps. 86:11). One would think it should be, "Teach me thy truth, and I will walk in thy way." But the reality is, it is the way of truth that God teaches and that we must choose to walk in. Christ is the way and the truth, and we must both learn Christ and walk in Him. We cannot walk in God's way and truth unless He teaches us, and if we expect Him to teach us, we must resolve to be governed by His teachings (Isa. 2:3).

David speaks of an upright heart: "Unite my heart to fear thy name" (v. 11). Make me sincere in religion. A hypocrite has a double heart; let mine be single and entire for God, not divided between Him and the world, not straying from Him. Our hearts are prone to wander and hang loose. Their powers and faculties wander after a thousand foreign things. We have need, therefore, of God's grace to unite them, that we may serve God with all that is within us, that we might be humbly employed in His service. Let my heart be fixed for God, and firm and faithful to Him, and fervent in serving Him. That is a united heart. (Henry, Matthew Henry's Commentary on the Whole Bible, pp. 867, 869)

36

Romans 15:4-6

As I have persisted in looking at this most interesting portion of Scripture, I must not allow the reader to depart from it without first exhorting him to the blessed conclusion the apostle has made of it, because it not only is applicable in the present instance but in every other where God the Holy Spirit leads His servants to make quotations from His holy Word in confirmation of His doctrines. The apostle says that whatsoever things were written before were written for our learning, that we through patience and comfort of the Scriptures might have hope. And the apostle adds a prayer that these blessed effects might follow in the church. Now then, from this passage we are authorized, as from many other parts of Scripture, to conclude that the whole body of the divine Word, as well as the prophecy of Scripture, is not of any private interpretation (2 Peter 1:20). Every part and portion of it is given with the express purpose, under the Almighty Author's teaching, of making the church wise unto salvation, through the faith which is in Christ Jesus. And God the Holy Spirit, from the continual and unceasing ministry of it in His church, is to make the church more and more acquainted with the person, character, offices, work, and glory of her right, lawful Lord. God the Holy

Spirit is continually accomplishing these great objects in the hearts of the Lord's redeemed ones by His gracious ministry. Reader, are you acquainted with these things? Do you give yourself wholly to them, in the concerns of salvation? Is Christ, in your view, all and in all? If so, it is the Lord the Holy Spirit who is your Teacher. For both by His personal ministry, as Jesus declared of Him, and by His written Word, He is the Lord who teaches you to profit (John 14:16–17). And you yourself become a living witness to this very scripture, that the God of patience and consolation has caused these things to be written for your learning, that you, through patience and comfort of the Scriptures, might have hope. (Hawker, Poor Man's New Testament Commentary, vol. 2, p. 350)

37

2 Corinthians 8:1-4

He commends the charity of the Macedonians and sets it forth with good advantage. He tells them that they were in a low condition, and in distress, yet they contributed to the relief of others. They were in great tribulation and deep poverty (v. 2). It was a time of great affliction with them, as may be seen in the record of Acts 18. The Christians in these parts had met with ill treatment, which had reduced them to deep poverty. Yet, as they had abundance of joy in the midst of tribulation, they abounded in their liberality. They gave out of the little they had, trusting in God to provide for them and make it up to them.

They gave very largely, with the riches of liberality; that is, as liberally as if they had been rich. It was a large contribution they made, all things considered. It was "according to, yea beyond, their power" (v. 3), as much as could well be expected from them, if not more. Note, though men may condemn the indiscretion, yet God will accept the pious zeal of those who in real works of piety and charity do things beyond their power.

They were very ready and eager to do this good work. "They were willing of themselves" and were so far from needing Paul to urge and press them with many arguments that they "prayed him with much entreaty to receive the gift" (v. 4). (Henry, Matthew Henry's Commentary on the Whole Bible, p. 2287)

38

Proverbs 15:1-2

Solomon, as conservator of the public peace, tells us here how the peace may be kept, that we may know how in our places to keep it: it is by soft words. If wrath rises like a threatening cloud, full of storms and thunder, a soft answer will disperse it and turn it away. When men are provoked, speak gently to them and give them good words, and they will be pacified, as the Ephraimites were by Gideon's mildness (Judg. 8:1–3). On another occasion, by Jephthah's roughness, they were exasperated, and the consequences were bad (Judg. 12:1–3). Reason will be better spoken, and a righteous cause better pleaded, with meekness than with passion; hard arguments do best with soft words.

If the peace is broken, may it be that we do nothing towards the breaking of it. Nothing stirs up anger and sows discord like grievous words, calling foul names such as *Raca* and "thou fool," or upbraiding men with their infirmities and infelicities, their extraction or education, or anything that lessens them and humiliates them. Scornful, spiteful reflections, by which men show their wit and malice, stir up the anger of others, which only increases and inflames their own anger. Rather than losing a jest, some will lose a friend and make an enemy. (Henry, Matthew Henry's Commentary on the Whole Bible, p. 987)

I should not think it necessary to make any break in the reading of these proverbs, were it not that the reader thereby may be prompted to pause here and there to ponder over the golden words and to gather from these precious sentences both spiritual and moral improvements from them. And the reader will find, if he makes a pause after every verse, more or less, that there is hardly one that, without violence to the expressions, doesn't carry with it a sweet gospel significance. And surely it is both gracious and blessed when we can thus bring with us the New Testament into the Old. Thus, for example, if we read the verses we have gone through in this passage, what can induce a soft answer to turn away wrath until our poor nature is regenerated and we have the Spirit of Christ? It is by the Spirit only, we are told, that we can "mortify the deeds of the body," and it is by His influences that we put off all these—"anger, wrath, malice, blasphemy, filthy communication out of our mouth" (Rom. 8:9–13; Col. 3:8). So, again, the proverb says that "the tongue of the wise useth knowledge aright" (Prov. 15:2). Yes, when the Lord has done by the sinner as by the prophet—laid the live coal taken from the holy altar upon his mouth and touched the lips—his iniquity is taken away and his sin is purged (Isa. 6:7). But without this, "who can bring a clean thing out of an unclean? not one" (Job 14:4). Reader, if we thus read the Proverbs through a gospel lens, we shall find words fitly spoken, "like apples of gold in pictures of silver" (Prov. 25:11). (Hawker, Poor Man's Old Testament Commentary, vol. 5, pp. 53–54)

39

Psalm 101

David speaks here concerning his conversation—concerning his conversation in general (how he would behave himself in everything: he would live by rule, and not at will, walking contrary to God; he would, though a king, by a solemn covenant bind himself to his good behavior) and concerning his conversation in his family particularly—not only how he would walk when he appeared in public, when he sat in the throne, but how he would walk within his house (v. 2), where he was more out of the eye of the world but where he still saw himself under the eye of God. It is not enough to put on our religion when we go out in public and appear before men; we must govern ourselves by it when we are with our families. Those who are in public offices are not thereby excused from carefulness in governing their families; rather, they are more concerned to set a good example of ruling their own houses well (1 Tim. 3:4). When David had his hands full of public affairs, he still returned to bless his own house (2 Sam. 6:20). He resolved to act conscientiously and with integrity, to walk in a perfect way, in the way of God's commandments, for "the law of the Lord is perfect" (Ps. 19:7). This he will walk in with a perfect heart (v. 2), with all sincerity, not being deceitful either with God or men. When we make the Word of God our rule (and are ruled by it) and make the glory of God our end (and aim at it), we walk in a perfect way with a perfect heart. To act considerately and with discretion, David says, "I will behave myself wisely." Some say, "I will understand or instruct myself in a perfect way. I will walk circumspectly." Note, we must all resolve to walk by the rules of Christian prudence, in the ways of Christian piety. We must never turn aside from the perfect way, pretending to behave wisely, but while we keep to the good way, we must be as wise as serpents. (Henry, Matthew Henry's Commentary on the Whole Bible, p. 887)

40

Matthew 5:13–16

See here, first, how our light must shine: by doing such good works as men may see and approve of, such works as are of good report among those who are outside the faith and will therefore give them cause to think well of Christianity. We must do good works that may be seen for the edification of others but not for our own boasting. We are called to pray in secret, and what happens between God and our souls must be kept to ourselves. But that which is of itself open and obvious to the sight of men we must work to make praiseworthy and in harmony with our profession (Phil. 4:8). Those around us must not only hear our good words but must also see our good works, that they may be convinced that religion is more than a bare name and that we do not only make a profession of it but abide under the power of it.

Secondly, observe for what end our light must shine: that those who see our good works may be brought not to glorify us (which was what the Pharisees aimed at, and it spoiled all their works) but to "glorify our Father which is in heaven" (v. 16). Note that the glory of God is the great thing we must aim for in everything we do in religion (1 Peter 4:11). In this center, the lines of all our actions must meet. We must not only endeavor to glorify God ourselves, but we must do all we can to bring others to glorify Him. The sight of our good works will do this by furnishing them with matters for praise. Let them see your good works, that they may see the power of God's grace in you and may thank Him for it and give Him the glory of it, who has given such power unto men. Our good works will also supply others with motives of piety. Let them see your good works, that they may be convinced of the truth and excellency of the Christian religion, may be provoked to imitate your good works in holiness, and so may glorify God. Note that the holy, regular, and exemplary conversation of the saints may do much towards the conversion of sinners; those who are unacquainted with religion may thereby be brought to know what it is. Examples teach. Those who are prejudiced against it may thereby by brought to being in love with it, and thus there is a winning virtue in godly conversation. (Henry, Matthew Henry's Commentary on the Whole Bible, p. 1631)

41

Psalm 11

All events are under the control of Providence. Consequently, all the trials of our outward life can be traced directly to the great First Cause [God]. Out of the golden gate of God's decrees, the armies of trial march forth in array, clad in their iron armor and armed with weapons of war. All providences are doors to trial. Even our mercies, like roses, have their thorns. Men may be drowned in seas of prosperity as well as in rivers of affliction. Our mountains are not too high, and our valleys are not too low for temptations: trials lurk on all roads. Everywhere, above and beneath, we are beset and surrounded with dangers. Yet no shower falls unpermitted from the threatening cloud; every drop of rain has its orders before it hastens to the earth. The trials which come from God are sent to prove and strengthen our graces and so at once to illustrate the power of divine grace, to test the genuineness of our virtues, and to add to their energy. Our Lord, in His infinite wisdom and superabundant love, sets so high a value upon His people's faith that He will not screen them from those trials by which faith is strengthened. You would never have possessed the precious faith which now supports you if the trial of your faith had not been so hot. You are a tree that never would have rooted so well if the wind had not rocked you back and forth and made you take firm hold on the precious truths of covenant grace. Worldly ease is a great foe to faith; it loosens the joints of holy valor and snaps the sinews of sacred courage. The balloon never rises until the cords are cut; affliction does this sharp service for believing souls. While the wheat sleeps comfortably in the husk, it is useless to man. It must be threshed out of its resting place before its value can be known. Thus, it is well that Jehovah tries the righteous, for it causes them to grow rich towards God. (Spurgeon, Morning and Evening: Daily readings, Morning, September 3)

42

Romans 4

The great gospel doctrine of justification by faith without the works of the law was so very contrary to the notions the Jews had learned from those who sat in Moses's chair that they could hardly swallow it. Therefore, the apostle insists on it and labors much in the confirmation and illustration of it. He had previously proved it by reason and argument; now in this chapter he proves it by example, which in some places serves for confirmation as well as illustration. The example he uses is that of Abraham, whom he chooses to mention because the Jews gloried much in their relation to Abraham and put it in the first rank of their external privileges that they were Abraham's seed and indeed had Abraham for their father. Therefore, this instance was likely to be more convincing to the Jews than any other. His argument stands thus: "All that are saved are justified in the same way as Abraham was; but Abraham was justified by faith and not by works; therefore, all that are saved are so justified." It would easily be acknowledged that Abraham was the father of the faithful. Now this is an argument not only *a pari*—from an equal case—but *a fortiori*, from a stronger case. If Abraham, a man so famous for works, so eminent in holiness and obedience, was nevertheless justified by faith only, and not by those works, how much less can any other, especially any of those that spring from him and come so far short of him in works, expect a justification by their own works? And it proves, likewise, *ex abundanti*—the more abundantly—that we are not justified by those good works which flow from faith, as the source of our righteousness, for such were Abraham's works, and are we better than he? The whole chapter is taken up with Paul's discourse upon this instance, and there is in it a particular reference to the close of the preceding chapter, where he has asserted that in the business of justification, Jews and Gentiles stand on the same level. Now in this chapter, with a great deal of strength of argument, he proves that Abraham was justified not by works but by faith. He observes when and why he was so justified. He describes and commends that faith of his. He applies all this to us. And if he had still been in the school of Tyrannus [see Acts 19:9], he could not have disputed more persuasively.

It is expressly said that Abraham's faith was counted to him for righteousness. What says the Scripture? In all controversies in religion this must be our question. It is not what this great man and the other good man say, but what says the Scripture? Ask counsel at this Abel and so end the matter (2 Sam. 20:18). To the law, and to the testimony (Isa. 8:20); there is the last appeal. Now the Scripture says that Abraham believed, and this was counted to him for righteousness (Gen. 15:6). Therefore, he had no reason to glory before God, it being purely of free grace that it was imputed and it not having in itself any of the formal nature of a righteousness, further than God Himself was graciously pleased so to count it to him. It is mentioned in Genesis on the occasion of a very conspicuous and remarkable act of faith concerning the promised seed and is the more notable in that it followed upon a grievous conflict Abraham had experienced with unbelief. His faith was now a victorious faith, newly returned from the battle. It is not perfect faith that is required for justification (there may be acceptable faith where there are remainders of unbelief) but prevailing faith, the faith that has the upper hand over unbelief. (Henry, Matthew Henry's Commentary on the Whole Bible, pp. 2201-2202)

43

Colossians 2:6-7

We see here a sovereign antidote against seducers: "As you have therefore received Christ Jesus the Lord, so walk you in him, rooted and built up..." (v. 6). Here note that all Christians have, in profession at least, "received Jesus Christ the Lord." We have received Him as Christ, the great Prophet of the church, anointed by God to reveal His will; received Him as Jesus, the great High Priest and Savior from sin and wrath by the expiatory sacrifice of Himself; and received Him as Lord, or Sovereign and King, whom we are to obey and be subject to. We have received Him, consented to Him, and taken Him for ours in every relation, in every capacity, and for all the purposes and uses of them.

The great concern of those who have received Christ is to walk in Him, to make their practices conformable to their principles and their conversation agreeable to their engagements. As we have received Christ, or consented to be His, so we must walk with Him in our daily lives and keep up our communion with Him.

The more closely we walk with Christ, the more we are "rooted and established in the faith" (v. 7). Good conduct is the best way to establish our faith. If we walk in Him, we shall be rooted in Him, and the more firmly we are rooted in Him, the more closely we shall walk in Him. "Rooted and built up." We cannot be built up in Christ unless we are first rooted in Him. We must be united to Him by a lively faith, and we must heartily consent to His covenant; then we shall grow up in Him in all things. "As you have been taught." This means according to the rule of the Christian doctrine in which you have been instructed. A good education has a good influence upon our establishment. We must be "established in the faith, as we have been taught, abounding therein." Being established in the faith, we must abound in it and improve in it more and more, and we must do this with thanksgiving. The way to have the benefit and comfort of God's grace is to be active in giving thanks for it. We must join thanksgiving to all our improvements and be sensible of the mercy of all our privileges and attainments. (Henry, Matthew Henry's Commentary on the Whole Bible, p. 2332)

44

Hebrews 4:14-16

See Him bearing our sicknesses and our sorrows. More than this, see Him carrying our iniquities and our sins. Think not that your path is an isolated one. The incarnate God has walked it before you, and He can give you the clear eye of faith to see His footprint in every step. Jesus can say, and He does say to you, "I know your sorrow; I know what that cross is, for I have carried it. You have not a burden that I did not bear, nor a sorrow that I did not feel, nor a pain that I did not endure, nor a path that I did not tread, nor a tear that did not moisten My eye, nor a cloud that did not shade My spirit before you, and for you. Is it bodily weakness? I once walked forty miles to carry the living water to a poor sinner at Samaria. Is it the sorrow of bereavement? I wept at the grave of my friend, although I knew that I was about to recall the loved one back again to life. Is it the frailty and the fickleness of human friendship? I stood by and heard Myself denied by lips that once spoke kindly to me, lips now renouncing me with an oath that once vowed affection unto death. Is it difficulty of circumstance, the galling sense of dependence? I was no stranger to poverty and was often nourished and sustained by the charity of others. Is it that you are houseless and friendless? So was I. The foxes have their shelter, and the birds their nests, but I, though Lord of all, had nowhere to lay My head, and often day after day passed away and no soothing accents of friendship fell upon My ear. Is it the burden of sin? Even that I bore in its accumulated and tremendous weight when I hung accursed upon the tree." (Winslow, Morning Thoughts, January 11)

45

Proverbs 22:9

Here is the description of a charitable man: he has a bountiful eye—opposed to the evil eye (Prov. 23:6) and synonymous with the single eye (Matt. 6:22). It is an eye that seeks out objects of charity, besides those that offer themselves; an eye that, upon the sight of one in need and misery, affects the heart with compassion; and an eye that, along with alms, gives a pleasant look, which makes the alms doubly acceptable. The charitable man also has a liberal hand: he gives of his bread—the bread appointed for his own eating—to those that need. He would rather short himself than see the poor perish for need, yet he does not give *all* his bread but *of* his bread; the poor shall have their share along with his own family.

We see here the blessedness of such a man. The loins of the poor will bless him, all about him will speak well of him, and God Himself will bless him in answer to many a good prayer put up for him. And thus he shall be blessed. (Henry, Matthew Henry's Commentary on the Whole Bible, p. 1004)

46

Psalm 34:18

There are those by whom a broken heart is despised. Satan despises it, though he trembles at it. The world despises it, though it stands in awe of it. The Pharisee despises it, though he attempts its counterfeit. But there is one who despises it not. "You will not despise it!" exclaims the penitent child, with his eye upon the loving heart of his God and Father. But why does God not only not despise it but also delights in and accepts it? Because He sees in it a holy and a fragrant sacrifice. It is a sacrifice, because it is offered to God and not to man. It is an offering laid upon His altar. Moses never presented such an offering; Aaron never offered such a sacrifice in all the gifts he offered, in all the victims he slew. And while some have cast their rich and splendid gifts into the treasury or have laid them ostentatiously upon the altar of Christian benevolence, God has stood by the spot to which some poor penitent has brought his broken heart for sin, the incense of which has gone up before Him as a most precious and fragrant sacrifice. Upon that offering, upon that gift, His eye has been fixed, as if one object, and one only, had captured and absorbed His gaze—it was a poor broken heart that lay bleeding and quivering upon His altar. It is a sacrifice, too, offered upon the basis of the atoning sacrifice of His dear Son—the only sacrifice that satisfies divine justice—and this makes it precious to God. So infinitely glorious is the atonement of Jesus, so divine, so complete, and so honoring to every claim of His moral government, that He accepts each sacrifice of prayer, of praise, of penitence, and of personal consecration laid in faith by the side and upon that one infinite sacrifice for sin. He recognizes in it, too, the work of His own Spirit. When the Spirit of God moved upon the face of unformed nature and a new world sprang into life, light, and beauty, He pronounced it very good. But what must be His estimate of that new creation which His Spirit has wrought in the soul, whose moral chaos He has transformed to life, light, and order!

But in what way does God demonstrate His satisfaction with, and His delight in, the broken and contrite heart? First, He manifests His power in healing it. "He heals the broken in heart, and binds up their wounds" (Ps. 147:3). "The Spirit of the Lord God is upon me; because the Lord has anointed me to preach good tidings to the meek: He has sent me to bind up the brokenhearted" (Isa. 61:1; Luke 4:18). Never did a physician delight more to display his skill or exercise the benevolent feelings of his nature in the alleviation of suffering than does Jesus in His work of binding up and healing the heart broken for sin by speaking a sense of pardon and applying to it the healing power of His own most precious blood. But our Lord doesn't only heal the contrite heart. As if heaven had not sufficient attraction as His dwelling-place, He comes down to earth and makes that heart His abode. "Thus says the high and lofty One, that inhabits eternity, whose name is Holy; I dwell in the high and holy place, with him also who is of a contrite and humble spirit, to revive the spirit of the humble, and to revive the heart of the contrite ones" (Isa. 57:15). What, dear, humble penitent, could give you such a view of the interest which Christ takes in your case, the delight with which He contemplates your contrition, and the welcome and the blessing which He is prepared to bestow upon you, on your casting yourself down at His feet, as this fact, that He waits to make that sorrow-stricken heart of yours His chief and loved abode—reviving it, healing it, and enshrining Himself forever within its renewed and sanctified affections. (Winslow, Evening Thoughts, January 7)

47

Luke 16:10–14

If we do not make a right use of the gifts of God's providence, how can we expect from Him those present and future comforts which are the gifts of His spiritual grace? Our Savior here compares these and shows that though our faithful use of the things of this world cannot be thought to merit any favor at the hand of God, yet our unfaithfulness in the use of them may be justly reckoned a forfeiture of that grace which is necessary to bring us to glory.

The riches of this world are the lesser; grace and glory are the greater. Now if we are unfaithful in the lesser, if we use the things of this world to other purposes than those for which they were given us, it may justly be feared that we should do so with the gifts of God's grace, that we should receive them also in vain, and therefore they will be denied to us: "He that is faithful in that which is least is faithful also in much" (v. 10). He that serves God and does good with his money will serve God and do good with the more noble and valuable talents of wisdom, grace, spiritual gifts, and the deposits of heaven. But he that buries the one talent of this world's wealth will never improve the five talents of spiritual riches. God withholds His grace from covetous, worldly people more than we are aware of.

The riches of this world are deceitful and uncertain; they are the unrighteous mammon which is hastening from us, and if we would make any advantage of it, we must rouse ourselves quickly. If we do not, how can we expect to be entrusted with spiritual riches, which are the only true riches? Let us be convinced of this: those are truly rich, and very rich, who are rich in faith, rich towards God, rich in Christ, and rich in the promises and the pledges of heaven. Let us therefore lay up our treasure in them, expect our portion from them, and keep first the kingdom of God and the righteousness thereof. And then, if other things be added to us, let us use them with a spiritual reference, so that by using them well we may take hold more quickly of the true riches and may be qualified to receive yet more grace from God. For God gives to a man what is good in His sight. To a free-hearted charitable man, He gives "wisdom, and knowledge, and joy" (Eccl. 2:26). To a man who is faithful in the unrighteous mammon, He gives the true riches.

The riches of this world are another man's; they are not our own, for they are foreign to the soul and its nature and interest. They are not our own, for they are God's; His title to them is prior and superior to ours. The ownership of them remains in Him; we are but the beneficiaries of them. They are another man's. We have them from others; we use them for others. What benefit has the owner from his goods that increase other than looking at them with his eyes? While they who eat of the world's riches are increased by them, they must soon leave them to others, and they know not to whom. But spiritual and eternal riches are inseparably our own (they enter into the soul that obtain them); they will never be taken away from us. If we make Christ our own, and the promises our own, and heaven our own, we have that which we may truly call our own. But how can we expect God to enrich us with these if we do not serve Him with our worldly possessions, of which we are but stewards?

We have no other way to prove ourselves the servants of God than by giving up ourselves so entirely to His service as to make mammon (that is, all our worldly gain) useful to us in His service. "No servant can serve two masters" (Matt. 6:24) whose commands are so inconsistent as those of God and mammon are. If a man will love the world and hold to it, it is necessary that he will hate God and despise Him. He will make all his pretensions of religion submit to his secular interests and designs, and the things of God shall be made to help him in serving and seeking the world. But on the other hand, if a man will love God and adhere to Him, he will comparatively hate the world (whenever God and the world come into competition) and despise it, making all his business and success in the world some way or other conducive to his furtherance in the business of religion. And the things of the world shall be made to help him in serving God and working out his salvation. The matter is laid plainly before us here: "Ye cannot serve God and mammon" (Matt. 6:24). So divided are their interests that their services can never be compounded. If, therefore, we are determined to serve God, we must disclaim and abandon the service of the world. (Henry, Matthew Henry's Commentary on the Whole Bible, p. 1882)

48

Colossians 3:23–24

To what imminent people was this word spoken? Was it to kings, who proudly boast a divine right? Ah, no! Too often, they serve themselves or Satan and forget the God whose patience permits them to wear their feigned majesty for their little hour. Does the apostle, then, speak to those so-called "right reverend fathers in God"—the bishops or "venerable archdeacons"? No, indeed! Paul knew nothing of these mere inventions of man. Not even to pastors and teachers, or to the wealthy and esteemed among believers, was this word spoken, but it was given to servants, yes, and to slaves. Among the toiling multitudes, the journeymen, the day laborers, the domestic servants, and the drudges of the kitchen, the apostle found, as we find still, some of the Lord's chosen. And to them he says, "Whatsoever ye do, do it heartily, as to the Lord, and not unto men; knowing that of the Lord ye shall receive the reward of the inheritance: for ye serve the Lord Christ." This saying gives honor to the weary routine of earthly employments and sheds a halo around the humblest occupations. To wash feet may be servile, but to wash His feet is royal work. To untie the shoestring is poor labor, but to untie the great Master's shoe is a princely privilege. The shop, the barn, the scullery, and the smithy become temples when men and women do all to the glory of God! Then, "divine service" is not a thing of a few hours and a few places, but all life becomes holiness unto the Lord and every place and thing as consecrated as the tabernacle and its golden candlestick.

"Teach me, my God and King, in all things thee to see;
And what I do in anything to do it as to thee.
All may of thee partake, nothing can be so mean,
Which with this tincture, for thy sake,
will not grow bright and clean.
A servant with this clause makes drudgery divine;
Who sweeps a room, as for thy laws,
makes that and the action fine."

(Spurgeon, Morning and Evening: Daily readings, Evening, December 11)

49

Titus 3:4-7

False grounds and motives are here removed: "Not by works of righteousness which we have done, but according to his mercy, he saved us" (v. 5); not for foreseen works of ours but His own free grace and mercy alone. Works must be in the saved man's life (where there is room for it), but not among the causes of his salvation. They are the way to the kingdom, not the meriting price of it; all is upon the principle of undeserved favor and mercy from first to last. Election is of grace: we are chosen to be holy, not because it was seen beforehand that we should be so (Eph. 1:4). It is the fruit, not the cause, of election. "God hath from the beginning chosen you to salvation through sanctification of the Spirit and belief of the truth" (2 Thess. 2:13). This is effectual calling, in which election breaks out and is first seen: He "hath saved us, and called us with a holy calling; not according to our works, but according to his own purpose and grace, which was given us in Christ Jesus before the world began" (2 Tim. 1:9). We are justified freely by grace (Rom. 3:24) and sanctified and saved by grace. "By grace you are saved, through faith; and that not of yourselves, it is the gift of God" (Eph. 2:8). Faith and all saving graces are God's free gift and His work; the beginning, increase, and perfection of them in glory are all from Him. In building men up to be a holy temple unto God, from the foundation to the capstone, we must cry nothing but "Grace, grace" unto it. It is not of works, lest any man should boast, but of grace, that he who glories should glory only in the Lord. Thus, the true cause is shown and the false removed. (Henry, Matthew Henry's Commentary on the Whole Bible, p. 2374)

50

Matthew 8:5-10

We have here an account of Christ's curing the centurion's servant of a palsy [paralysis]. This was done at Capernaum, where Christ was living (Matt. 4:13). Christ went about doing good and came home to do good too; every place He came to was the better for His being there.

Observe the centurion's great faith. The more humility, the more faith; the more modest we are of ourselves, the stronger will be our confidence in Jesus Christ. He had an assurance of faith not only that Christ could cure his servant but that He could cure him from a distance. There was no need for any physical contact, as in natural operations, nor any application to the part affected. But the cure, he believed, might be administered without bringing the physician and patient together. We read afterwards of those who brought the man sick of the palsy to Christ, through much difficulty, and set him before Him. And Christ commended their faith for a working faith. This centurion did not bring his man sick of the palsy, and Christ commended his faith as a trusting faith: true faith is accepted of Christ, regardless of how it manifests itself. Christ has the best interpretation of the different methods of [true] religion that people take and thereby has taught us to do so too. This centurion believed, and it is undoubtedly true, that the power of Christ knows no limits, and therefore nearness and distance are alike to Him. Distance of place cannot obstruct either the knowing or working of Him who fills all places. "Am I a God at hand, says the Lord, and not a God afar off" (Jer. 23:23)?

The centurion believed Jesus could cure his servant with a word, not send him a medicine (much less a charm) but only speak the word. He did not doubt that his servant would be healed. Herein he acknowledges Jesus to have a divine power, an authority to command all the creatures and powers of nature, which enables Him to do whatever He pleases in the kingdom of nature, just as at first He raised that kingdom by an almighty word when He said, "Let there be light." With men, saying and doing are two things. But not so with Christ, who is therefore the Arm of the Lord, because He is the eternal Word. His saying "Be ye warmed and filled" (Jas. 2:16) brought healing and warmth, filling and healing. (Henry, Matthew Henry's Commentary on the Whole Bible, pp. 1648-1649)

51

1 Corinthians 14:20

He adds a plain proclamation that the fondness then discovered for this gift [speaking in tongues] was too clear an indication of the immaturity of their judgment: "Brethren, be not children in understanding; in malice be you children, but in understanding be men." Children are apt to be struck with novelty and strange appearances. They are taken with an outward show, without looking into the true nature and worth of things. Do not act like them and prefer noise and show to worth and substance; show a greater maturity of judgment and act a more manly part—be like children in nothing but an innocent and inoffensive disposition. A double rebuke is couched in this passage, both of their pride on account of their gifts and their arrogance and haughtiness towards each other, with the contests and quarrels that proceed from them. Note, Christians should be as harmless and inoffensive as children, void of all guile and malice, but they should have wisdom and knowledge that are ripe and mature. They should not be "unskillful in the word of righteousness" (Heb. 5:13), though they should be unskillful in all the arts of mischief. (Henry, Matthew Henry's Commentary on the Whole Bible, p. 2270)

52

James 1:22–27

Nothing can be more evident from the whole scope of James's epistle, taken in one mass of particulars, than that he is admonishing the real church of God—made up of true, regenerated believers—against the nominal church of professors, in whose hearts no saving change had been wrought. There were in this apostle's days, as there have been in all ages of the church as well as in our days, vain talkers, whose religion consisted only in name. We read of such in Hebrews 6:4–6 and Titus 1:10–16. And James, through the whole of this epistle, is continually speaking of these nominal Christians by way of instructing the Lord's people. I beg the reader to pause over the apostle's expression "the perfect law of liberty" (v. 25). What can be meant by it other than the person and work of Christ? The engrafted Word [the Scriptures] and the uncreated Word [Jesus Christ] are those mirrors here referred to, into which by looking we behold the Lord's perfections for His people. Paul has a similar figure. "But we all, with open face beholding as in a glass the glory of the Lord, are changed into the same image, from glory to glory, even as by the Spirit of the Lord" (2 Cor. 3:18). Here, as in James, the church of true children, regenerated and made new creatures in Christ Jesus, are considered as looking wholly to Jesus. And thus, looking under the Spirit's influence (for where the Spirit of the Lord is, there is liberty) to Jesus, they imbibe His graces, are made to imitate His example, and delight in all that belongs to Him and the holy principles of His gospel. This is the life of God's child: a doer of the word and not a hearer only. In contradiction, the nominal professor knows these things only by name. And although he may observe the greatest punctuality in attending divine ordinances, where the heart is not regenerated, head knowledge is in vain. The love of Christ is only known, and felt, and enjoyed in the renewed man. Where this is wanting, all is wanting. Where God the Spirit has wrought the saving change, all acts of grace, more or less, will follow. And it isn't just the purity of those principles, begotten by regeneration, that will show themselves in the life and conversation, in visiting the fatherless and widows in their affliction. Through the Spirit, the child of God will be enabled to "mortify the deeds of the body" (Rom. 8:13) and will be kept from "mingling with the heathen, and learning their works" (Ps. 106:35). (Hawker, Poor Man's New Testament Commentary, vol. 3, pp. 325–326)

53

Deuteronomy 15:7–8

Reader, dwell particularly on those endearing words "thy brother" while reading this precept. Then, turn your thoughts to Jesus, a brother born for adversity, and call to mind that, in every instance of a real brother in Jesus who is in distress, he is His image and is His representative (Matt. 25:40). Read that scripture with this one, and may God the Holy Spirit give energy to it, both in your mind and mine. Few have ever entered into the full meaning of it. (Hawker, Poor Man's Old Testament Commentary, vol. 2, p. 80)

54

Romans 12:3–5

One of the most delightful of all thoughts, and one which when fully enjoyed under the influence of the Holy Spirit gives an unspeakable felicity in the heart, is of that union and fellowship of Christ with His church. Ponder it, my soul, this morning. All the members of Christ's body are one body, the apostle says, in Christ, and He is the head over all things to the church, "which is his body, the fulness of him that filleth all in all" (Eph. 1:23). I would never, if possible, lose sight of this, because in the perfect conviction and assurance of it must be found all our security and joy. And the way by which this blessed truth, under divine teaching, will be kept alive in the soul is this: I would consider what I am by nature and practice in Adam and connect to this view what I am by grace and faith in Christ. Now, as Adam was the common head of all his seed in nature, equally so is Christ the common head of all His seed in grace. Do I consider that when Adam sinned in the garden, I as one of his children (as Scripture says of Levi, in respect to his connection with Abraham) was in his loins, part of him, and consequently implicated and involved in all the good or bad belonging to him? Then it will follow that in Adam's sin, I sinned, and in Adam's condemnation, I was included. So then, as Adam did not transgress only for himself but for all his seed by nature that should come from him, equally so when Christ fulfilled all righteousness, and when Christ expiated all sin by the sacrifice of Himself, His seed were considered righteous in Him. And His expiatory sacrifice, as the head of His people, must be, to all intents and purposes, the same as if they had been sacrificed with Him. Cherish this thought, my soul, and never allow yourself to behold Christ as the Christ of God in the capacity of a private or single person but as the covenant head, the Father's chosen, the sent, the sealed, the anointed of God in whom all His members are one body in Christ. See that you have the Spirit of Christ, by which you are proved to be one of His! And for the full enjoyment of all the blessings contained in this union and communion with your glorious head, daily and hourly remind God your Father of all His covenant promises made to Christ as the head of His church and people, of which the Lord has said, "I will pour my Spirit upon thy seed, and my blessing upon thine offspring" (Isa. 44:3). (Hawker, The Poor Man's Morning Portion, July 29)

55

Proverbs 2:6–7

God has wisdom to bestow. The Lord not only is wise Himself, but He gives wisdom, and that is more than the wisest men in the world can do, for it is God's prerogative to open the understanding. All the wisdom that is in any creature is His gift—His free gift—and He gives it liberally (James 1:5), has given it to many, and is still giving it. To Him, therefore, let us apply for it.

He has blessed the world with a revelation of His will. Out of His mouth, by the law and the prophets, by the written Word and His ministers (both of which are His mouth to the children of men) come knowledge and understanding, such a discovery of truth and good as, if we admit and receive the impressions of it, will make us truly knowing and intelligent. It is both an engagement and encouragement for us to search after wisdom that we have the Scriptures to search, in which we may find it if we seek it diligently. (Henry, Matthew Henry's Commentary on the Whole Bible, p. 958)

56

Ephesians 2:7–10

This chapter contains an account of the miserable condition the Ephesians were in by nature, the glorious change that was wrought in them by converting grace, and the great and mighty privileges that both converted Jews and Gentiles receive from Christ.

Observe what is the great design and aim of God in producing and bringing about this change: "That in the ages to come he might show," that He might give a specimen and proof of His great goodness and mercy for the encouragement of sinners in future time. Observe that the goodness of God in converting and saving sinners in times past is a proper encouragement to those who come later to hope in His grace and mercy and to apply themselves to these. God having this in His design, poor sinners should take great encouragement from it. And what shouldn't we hope for from such grace and kindness, from riches of grace, to which this change is owing? With respect to regenerated sinners themselves, their regeneration has come through Christ Jesus, by and through whom God conveys all His favor and blessings to us. "For we are his workmanship, created in Christ Jesus unto good works" (v. 10). It appears that all is of grace, because all our spiritual advantages are from God. We are His workmanship in respect of the new creation, not only as men but also as saints. The new man is a new creature, and God is his Creator. It is a new birth, and we are born, or begotten, of His will. This occurs "in Christ Jesus"; that is, on the account of what He has done and suffered and by the influence and operation of His blessed Spirit. This regeneration is "unto good works." The apostle has previously ascribed this change to divine grace in exclusion of works. Lest he should seem thereby to discourage good works, he here observes that though the change is to be ascribed to nothing of that nature (for we are the workmanship of God), yet God, in His new creation, has designed and prepared us for good works, "created unto good works," with a design that we should be fruitful in them. Wherever God by His grace implants good principles, they are intended to be for good works. These are works "which God hath before ordained"; that is, decreed and appointed. Or the words may be read, "To which God hath before prepared us, that is, by blessing us with the knowledge of his will, and with the assistance of his Holy Spirit; and by producing such a change in us." Why did God ordain these good works? "That we should walk in them," or glorify God by exemplary conduct and by our perseverance in holiness. (Henry, Matthew Henry's Commentary on the Whole Bible, pp. 2309–2310)

57

Hebrews 10

The apostle knew very well that the Hebrews to whom he wrote were strangely fond of the Levitical dispensation, and therefore he fills his mouth with arguments to wean them from it. To do this, he proceeds in this chapter to lay low the whole of that priesthood and sacrificial system. He raises and exalts the priesthood of Christ very high, that he might effectually recommend Him and His gospel to them. He shows to believers the honors and dignities of their regenerated state and calls them to suitable duties.

The apostle tells us the way and means by which Christians enjoy such privileges and, in general, declares it to be by the blood of Jesus, by the merit of that blood which He offered up to God as an atoning sacrifice. He has purchased for all who believe in Him free access to God in the ordinances of His grace here and in the kingdom of His glory. This blood, being sprinkled on the conscience, chases away slavish fear and gives the believer assurance of both his safety and his welcome into the divine presence.

Now the apostle, having given this general account of the way by which we have access to God, enters further into the particulars of it. He tells them it is the only way; there is no way left but this. The first way to the Tree of Life is, and has been, long sealed up.

It is a new way, in opposition to both the covenant of works and the antiquated dispensation of the Old Testament. It is *via novissima*—the last way that will ever be opened to men. Those who will not enter in this way exclude themselves forever. It is a way that will always be effectual.

It is a living way. It would be death to attempt to come to God in the way of the covenant of works, but by this way, we may come to God and live. It is by a living Savior, who, though He was dead, is alive, and it is a way that gives life and lively hope to those who enter into it.

It is a way that Christ has consecrated for us through the veil; that is, His flesh. The veil in the tabernacle and temple signified the body of Christ. When He died, the veil of the temple was torn in two, and this was at the time of the evening sacrifice, giving the people a surprising view into the Holy of Holies, which they had never seen before. Our way to heaven is by a crucified Savior; His death is to us the way of life. To those who believe this, He will be precious. (Henry, Matthew Henry's Commentary on the Whole Bible, pp. 2395-2396)

58

1 Corinthians 2:6–16

R eader, behold the great apostle in his fervent zeal for the cross of Christ! Think in what view that cross appeared to his mind! He knew its value. He had felt, and experienced, the blessedness of it to his own soul, and as such, he could not remain silent in holding it forth to others. His own weakness and feebleness in preaching Christ and Him crucified, he considered as nothing, while he kept in remembrance that divine strength was rendered the more conspicuous in human nothingness. Indeed, the apostle rejoiced in the awareness that the more feeble his ministry was in itself, the more evident would appear Christ's glory: their faith was found not to stand in the wisdom of man but in the power of God.

Blessed be God the Holy Spirit for the sweet instruction communicated to the church in this precious chapter! Yes, almighty Teacher, we do find cause to bless You for the very clear and decisive line You have drawn between natural knowledge and divine, between the wisdom which is from beneath and that which is from above. None, indeed, of the princes of this world knew the Lord of glory. Neither will they ever, by mere human intellect, discover the hidden wisdom of God. But while these things are hidden from the wise and prudent, oh the graciousness of our God to reveal them to babes! Lord, may Your people know their sonship and adoption character by Your divine instruction, and may we have all grace, while You are condescending to be our Teacher, to know the things which are freely given to us of God, comparing spiritual things with spiritual. (Hawker, Poor Man's New Testament Commentary, vol. 2, p. 381)

59

Hebrews 6:11–12

The doctrine of an assured belief of the pardon of sin, of acceptance in Christ, and of adoption into the family of God has been, and continues to be, regarded by many as an attainment never to be expected in the present life. And when it is expressed, it is viewed with a suspicion unfavorable to the character of the work. But this is contrary to the divine Word and to the concurrent experience of millions who have lived and died in the full assurance of hope. The doctrine of assurance is a doctrine of undoubted revelation, implied and expressed. That it is enforced as a state of mind essential to the salvation of the believer, we cannot admit. But that it is insisted upon as essential to his comfortable and holy walk, and as greatly involving the glory of God, we must strenuously maintain. Else why these marked references to the doctrine? In Colossians 2:1–2, Paul expresses "great conflict" for the saints, that their "hearts might be comforted, being knit together in love, and unto all riches of the full assurance of understanding." In the epistle to the Hebrews, he exhorts them, "Let us draw near with a true heart in full assurance of faith" (Heb. 10:22), with similar language in our motto. To crown all, the apostle Peter thus earnestly exhorts, "Wherefore the rather, brethren, give diligence to make your calling and election sure" (2 Peter 1:10). We trust no further proof from the sacred Word is required to authenticate the doctrine. It is written as with a sunbeam: "The Spirit itself bears witness with our spirit, that we are the children of God" (Rom. 8:15–17).

It is the duty and the privilege of every believer diligently and prayerfully to seek the sealing of the Spirit. A man stops short of his great privilege if he slights or undervalues this blessing. Do not be satisfied with the faint impression which you received in conversion. In other words, do not rest content with a past experience. Many are satisfied with a mere hope that they once passed from death unto life, and with this feeble and, in many cases, doubtful evidence they are content to pass all their days and to go down to the grave. Ah, reader, if you are really converted and your soul is in a healthy, growing, spiritual state, you will want more than this. And especially, too, if you are led into deeper self-knowledge—a more intimate acquaintance with the roughness of the rough way and the straightness of the straight path—you will want a present Christ to lean upon and to live upon. Past experience will not do for you, save only as it confirms your soul in the faithfulness of God. "Forgetting those things that are behind" (Phil. 3:13), you will seek a present pardon, a present sense of acceptance. And the daily question, as you near your eternal home, will be, "How do I now stand with God? Is Jesus precious to my soul now? Is He my daily food? What do I experience of daily visits from and to Him? Do I more and more see my own vileness, emptiness, and poverty and His righteousness, grace, and fullness? And should the summons now come, am I ready to depart and to be with Christ?" As you value a happy and a holy walk, as you would be jealous for the honor and glory of the Lord, as you wish to be the "salt of the earth," the "light of the world" (Matt. 5:13–16), as you wish to be a savor of Christ in every place—oh, seek the sealing of the Spirit! Rest not short of it; reach after it; press towards it. It is your duty. Oh, that the duty may be your privilege! Then shall you exclaim with an unfaltering tongue, "Abba, Father!" "My Lord, and my God!" (Winslow, Evening Thoughts, May 19)

60

Psalm 131

It is a paradox to men of the world, but the fact is undeniable that the soul when most humble is most bold; he that is most depressed is most exalted; most empty and yet most full. For he that has the lowest views of his own merit has the highest views of Christ. And he that has learned the first lesson in the school of grace—to be most humbled under a sense of sin—will be most bold to plead Christ and His righteousness. Neither can a child of God be properly prepared to receive out of Christ's fullness until he is self-emptied and comes with nothing, that he may receive all. The figure of a weaned child is beautifully chosen to represent this, for as our Lord taught, except we be weaned and become as little children, desirous to be taught everything because we know nothing, we shall be as wayward and perverse as babes at the full breast of an indulgent mother (Matt. 18:3). Lord, give me this weaned state, that I may hang upon the God of Israel, even a God in Christ forever! (Hawker, Poor Man's Old Testament Commentary, vol. 4, p. 596)

61

John 11:1–10

In this passage, we see Jesus desiring to go into Judea upon hearing of Lazarus's sickness. The disciples protest that the Jews are seeking to do Him harm. Christ's answer to this objection is, "Are there not twelve hours in the day?" How did He reckon the hours of daylight? According to some, the Jews divided every day into twelve hours and made their hours longer or shorter according as the days were, so that an hour with them was the twelfth part of the time between sun and sun. Another possibility is that, lying much more south than we, their days were closer to twelve hours long than ours. The divine Providence has given us daylight to work by, and He lengthens it out to a reasonable amount of time. Looking at the entire year, every country has just as much daylight as night, not counting the twilight times. Man's life is a day; this day is divided into various ages, states, and opportunities, such as shorter or longer hours, as God has appointed. The consideration of this should make us not only very busy in the work of life (if there are twelve hours in the day, each of them ought to be filled up with duty and none of them trifled away) but also very much at ease as to the perils of life. Our day shall be lengthened out till our work is done and our testimony is finished. Christ applies this principal to the present case and shows why He must go to Judea: because He had a clear call to go.

First, He shows the comfort and satisfaction which a man has in his own mind while he keeps in the way of his duty, as it is generally prescribed by the Word of God and particularly determined by the providence of God. "If any man walk in the day, he stumbles not" (v. 9); that is, if a man keeps focused on his duty, minding that and setting the will of God before him as his rule, with an impartial respect to all God's commandments, he does not hesitate in his own mind, but, walking uprightly, he walks surely and with a holy confidence. As he that walks in the day does not stumble but goes on steadily and cheerfully in his way because he sees the light of this world and by it sees his way before him, so a good man, without any other security or sinister aims, relies upon the Word of God as his rule. He regards the glory of God as his end, because he sees those two great lights [the Word of God and his duty] and keeps his eye upon them. Thus, he is furnished with a faithful guide in all his doubts and a powerful guard in all his dangers (Gal. 6:4; Ps. 119:6). Wherever Christ went, He walked in the day, and so shall we, if we follow in His steps.

Second, He shows the pain and peril a man is in who walks not according to this rule: "If a man walk in the night, he stumbles" (v. 10); that is, if a man walks in the way of his heart, and the sight of his eyes, and according to the course of this world—if he consults his own carnal reasonings more than the will and glory of God—he falls into temptations and snares, is liable to great uneasiness and frightful apprehensions, trembles at the shaking of a leaf, and flees when no one pursues. An upright man, on the other hand, laughs at the shaking of the spear and stands undaunted when ten thousand invade (Isa. 33:14–16). A man walking in the night stumbles because there is no light in him, for light *in* us is to our moral actions what light *around* us is to our natural actions. He doesn't have a good principle within; he is not sincere; his eye is evil. Thus, Christ not only justifies in this passage His purpose of going into Judea but also encourages His disciples to go along with Him, fearing no evil. (Henry, Matthew Henry's Commentary on the Whole Bible, p. 1989)

62

Ephesians 4:29

We are here warned against corrupt communication and directed to that which is useful and edifying. Filthy and unclean words and discourse are poisonous and infectious, like putrid, rotten meat. They proceed from and prove a great deal of corruption in the heart of the speaker and tend to corrupt the minds and manners of others who hear them; therefore, Christians should beware of all such discourse. It may be taken as true for all that which provokes the lusts and passions of others. We must not only put off corrupt communications but put on "that which is good to the use of edifying." The great use of speech is to edify those with whom we speak. Christians should endeavor to promote a useful conversation "that it may minister grace unto the hearers" and that it may be good for, and acceptable to, the hearers in the way of information, counsel, pertinent reproof, or the like. It is the great duty of Christians to take care that they do not offend with their lips and that they improve discourse and conversation as much as may be for the good of others. (Henry, Matthew Henry's Commentary on the Whole Bible, p. 2315)

63

James 4:8-10

"Draw nigh to God." We have great encouragement to act thus towards God: He will draw nigh to those that draw nigh to Him, and He will lift up those who humble themselves in His sight. Those who draw nigh to God in a way of duty shall find God drawing nigh to them in a way of mercy. Draw nigh to Him in faith, trust, and obedience, and He will draw nigh to you for your deliverance. If there is not a close communion between God and us, it is our fault and not His. He shall lift up the humble. Our Lord Himself declared, "He that shall humble himself shall be exalted" (Matt. 23:12). If we are truly penitent and humble under the marks of God's displeasure, we shall soon know the advantages of His favor. He will lift us up out of trouble, or He will lift us up in our spirits and comforts under trouble. He will lift us up to honor and safety in the world, or He will lift us up in our way to heaven, so as to raise our hearts and affections above the world. God will "revive the spirit of the humble" (Isa. 57:15), He will hear the desire of the humble (Ps. 10:17), and He will at last lift them up to glory. Before honor comes humility. The highest honor in heaven will be the reward of the greatest humility on earth. (Henry, Matthew Henry's Commentary on the Whole Bible, p. 2417)

64

1 Corinthians 7:20–24

The apostle makes use of the same kind of reasoning in these verses as he did on the subject of circumcision (vv. 17–19). Here, he speaks concerning the various areas of social life: the servant with the master, the wife with her husband, and, in short, all the various callings of the world. All situations in civil society, provided the occupation is lawful and honest, may be followed, for they have nothing to do with the grand concerns of salvation. He that is called in the Lord with a holy calling by sovereign grace and is thereby proved to be of the family of Christ, bought with the precious price of Christ's blood and redeemed from the fallen nature of Adam, has an infinitely higher concern than the mere consideration of any worldly calling. The time here is short. It is hardly worth a thought what station of life a man is placed in—high or low, rich or poor—unless it is so that he might seek that which might best promote the everlasting interests of the upper and brighter world. Even with the fond relationships of our lives, our continuance in them is so short-lived that we ought to sit as loose and detached from them as possible, remembering that, as we have no continuing city here, we ought to be always on the lookout for one to come (Heb. 13:14). (Hawker, Poor Man's New Testament Commentary, vol. 2, p. 416)

65

Luke 23:39-43

M y soul, hear the gracious words of Jesus! This was the third cry of the Redeemer from the cross. And oh, how full of grace—rich, free, unmerited, unexpected, unlooked-for grace—they are to a poor, lost, perishing sinner, even in the very moment of death. Let the self-righteous Pharisee behold this example of redeeming love and let him wonder and be confounded. Surely no one will venture to suppose that this man's good works were any recommendation, when the poor wretch was dying under the hands of justice. What was it, then, that saved him but the complete salvation of Jesus? The Son of God was offering to this man's soul on the cross a sacrifice for sin and, being between two notorious sinners, gave a rich display of the sovereignty of His grace and His love to poor sinners. In confirmation of that love, He snatched this one as a brand from the burning—took him from the very jaws of hell—and that very day led him in triumph to heaven, thereby manifesting to every poor sinner in whose heart He puts the cry for mercy that that cry shall never be put forth in vain. And mark, my soul, how powerfully the grace of the Lord Jesus worked upon this man. He and his companion both knew that before night they would be in eternity. The thought affected neither; they joined the rabble in insulting Jesus. "Save Yourself and us" was the language of the heart of both, until the grace of Jesus worked on this man's mind and changed the reviler into a humble petitioner. What could there be in Jesus thus to affect him? Jesus hung upon the cross like a poor Jew. Jesus had always been poor, and never more so than now. And yet, in the midst of all these surrounding circumstances, such a ray of light broke in upon this man's mind that he saw Jesus in all His glory and power, acknowledged Him as a king when all the disciples had forsaken Him and fled, and prayed to be remembered by Him when He came into His kingdom. Precious Lamb of God! Give me such a portion of Your grace that I, under all the unpromising circumstances around me, may call forth the same conviction of Your power and my need. And oh, that this pattern of mercy might be reviewed by thousands of poor perishing, dying sinners. I would have it proclaimed through all the public gathering places, through all the haunts of licentiousness, among the numberless scenes of hardened sinners who fear that they have sinned beyond the possibility of forgiveness. Oh, look at this example of Jesus's love, you that are going down to the grave full of sin and despair. Behold the thief; behold the Savior! And oh, for a cry of grace like that of the dying malefactor, "Lord, remember me when thou comest into thy kingdom" (v. 42)! And then to hear Jesus's gracious answer, "Today shalt thou be with me in paradise" (v. 43). (Hawker, The Poor Man's Morning Portion, April 11)

66

John 14:27-28

Peace is also a fruit of spiritual-mindedness. What peace of conscience does that individual possess whose mind is stayed upon spiritual things! It is as much the reward as it is the effect of his cultivated heavenliness. The existence of this precious blessing, however, supposes the exposure of the spiritual mind to much that has a tendency to ruffle and disturb its composure and tranquility. The Christian is far from being entirely exempt from those irritations and anxieties which seem inseparable from human life. To the brooding anxieties arising from external things—life's difficulties, changes, and disappointments—there are added those things that are peculiar to the child of God, the internal things that distract—the cloudings of guilt, the agitations of doubt, the corrodings of fear, the mourning of penitence, the discipline of love.

But through all this there flows a river, the streams of which make glad the city of God (Ps. 46:4). It is the peace of the heavenly mind, the peace which Jesus procured, which God imparts and which the Holy Spirit seals. A heavenly mind soars above a poor dying world, living not upon a creature's love or smile, casting its daily need upon the heart of a kind Providence, being anxious for nothing but with supplication and thanksgiving making known its requests unto God (Phil. 4:6), being indifferent to the turmoil, vexations, and checkered scenes of worldly life, and living in simple faith and seeking to please Christ. Detached from earth and moving heavenwards by the attractions of its peaceful coast, it realizes a peace which passes all understanding (Phil 4:7).

And if this is the present state of the heavenly mind, what will be the future of the mind in heaven? Heaven is the abode of perfect peace. There are no cloudings of guilt, no tossings of grief, no agitations of fear, no corrodings of anxiety there. It is the peace of perfect purity; it is the rest of complete satisfaction. It is not so much the entire absence of all sorrow as it is the actual presence of all holiness that constitutes the charm and the bliss of future glory.

The season of sorrow is frequently converted into that of secret joy, Christ making our very griefs to sing. But the occasion of sin is always that of bitter grief; our backslidings often, like scorpions, entwine around our hearts. If there were ever (as most assuredly there will not be) sadness in heaven, there might still be the accompaniment of happiness. But if there were sin in heaven—the shadow of a shade of guilt—it would obscure and embitter all. Thus, as heaven is the abode of perfect peace, he who on earth has his conduct most in heaven approximates in his feelings the nearest condition to the heavenly state. Oh, that our hearts were more yielding to the sweet, holy, and powerful attractions of the heavenly world! Then would our actions be more in heaven. (Winslow, Morning Thoughts, August 7)

67

John 14:25–26

Oh, blessed Spirit, to whom I owe such unspeakable mercies! Let me, Lord, contemplate You this day under this gracious, kind, compassionate office of the Comforter. You are indeed the Holy Spirit, the Comforter. And how mercifully do You sympathize with all the followers of Jesus in their various afflictions, both of soul and body! How tenderly do You show us our sins and lead us to Jesus's blood to wash them away! How sweetly do You visit, encourage, strengthen, instruct, lead, and guide us into all truth! And how powerfully, at times, by Your restraining grace, do You enable us to mortify the deeds of the body that we may live! Hail, holy, blessed, almighty Comforter! Oh, let Your visits be continual! Come, Lord, and abide with me, and be with me forever. Manifest that You are the sent one of the Father and of the Son in coming to me in Jesus's name, in teaching me of all the precious things concerning Jesus, and in reminding me always of Jesus. Do all this so that in You and by Your blessed work I may know and live in the sweet enjoyment of fellowship with the Father and with His Son, Jesus Christ, through the influences of You, the Holy Spirit, the Comforter! (Hawker, The Poor Man's Morning Portion, November 2)

68

Psalm 27

It may seem an easy thing to wait, but it is one of the postures which a Christian soldier learns only with years of teaching. Marching and quick-marching are much easier for God's warriors than standing still. There are hours of perplexity when the most willing spirit, anxiously desirous to serve the Lord, knows not what part to take. Then what shall it do? Worry itself through despair? Fly back in cowardice, turn to the right hand in fear, or rush forward in presumption? No, but simply wait. Wait in *prayer*, however. Call upon God and spread the matter before Him; tell Him your difficulty and plead His promise of aid. In dilemmas between one duty and another, it is sweet to be humble as a child and to wait with simplicity of soul upon the Lord. It is sure to be well with us when we feel and know our own folly and are heartily willing to be guided by the will of God. But wait in *faith*. Express your steady confidence in Him, for unfaithful, untrusting waiting is an insult to the Lord. Believe that even if He keeps you tarrying till midnight, He will come at the right time; the vision shall come and shall not tarry. Wait in *quiet patience*, not rebelling because you are under the affliction but blessing your God for it. Never murmur against the second cause, as the children of Israel did against

Moses. Never wish you could go back to the world again, but accept the case as it is and put it—as it stands, simply and with your whole heart, without any self-will—into the hand of your covenant God, saying, "Now, Lord, not my will but Yours be done. I know not what to do; I am brought to hardships, but I will wait until You shall part the waters or drive back my foes. I will wait, if You keep me many days, for my heart is fixed upon You alone, O God, and my spirit waits for You in the full conviction that You will yet be my joy and my salvation, my refuge and my strong tower." (Spurgeon, Morning and Evening: Daily readings, Morning, August 30)

Note: Some think David penned this psalm before his coming to the throne, when he was in the midst of his troubles, and perhaps upon occasion of the death of his parents. But the Jews think he penned it when he was old, upon occasion of the wonderful deliverance he had from the sword of the giant [Ishbibenob], when Abishai protected him (2 Sam. 21:16, 17) and his people resolved he should never risk his life again in battle, lest he should quench the light of Israel. Perhaps it was not penned upon any particular occasion. But it is very expressive of the pious and devout affections with which gracious souls are carried out towards God at all times, especially in times of trouble. (Henry, Matthew Henry's Commentary on the Whole Bible, pp. 778–779)

69

Galatians 5:13-23

In the latter part of this chapter, the apostle comes to exhort these Christians to serious practical godliness as the best antidote against the snares of the false teachers.

It is necessary that they should not strive with one another but love one another. He tells them that they have been called unto liberty, and he would have them to stand firm in the liberty through which Christ has made them free. But he would nonetheless have them be very careful that they did not use this liberty as an occasion to the flesh, that they did not take the opportunity to indulge themselves in any corrupt affections and practices and particularly such as might create distance and disaffection and be the ground of quarrels and contentions among them. On the contrary, he would have them by love to serve one another, to maintain that mutual love and affection which, notwithstanding any minor differences there might be among them, would dispose them to all that respect and kindness towards each other which the Christian religion obliges them to.

Note, the liberty we enjoy as Christians is not a licentious liberty. Though Christ has redeemed us from the curse of the law, He has not freed us from the obligation of it. The gospel is a "doctrine according to godliness" (1 Tim. 6:3) and is so far from giving the least support to sin that it lays us under the strongest obligations to avoid and subdue it. Though we ought to stand fast in our Christian liberty, we should not insist upon it to the disruption of Christian love. We should not use it as an occasion for strife and contention with our fellow Christians who may be differently minded from us. Instead, we should always maintain such an attitude towards each other as may dispose us by love to serve one another. To this the apostle endeavors to persuade these Christians, and there are two considerations which he sets before them for this purpose. "All the law is fulfilled in one word, even in this, Thou shalt love thy neighbor as thyself" (v. 14). Love is the sum of the whole law. As love to God summarizes the duties of the first table, so love to our neighbor is the focus of the second. The apostle takes notice of the latter here, because he is speaking of their behavior towards one another. And when he makes use of this as an argument to persuade them to mutual love, he indicates that this would be both a good evidence of their sincerity in religion and also the most likely means of rooting out those dissensions and divisions that were among them. It will become evident that we are truly the disciples of Christ when we have "love one to another" (John 13:35), and where this attitude is kept up, if it doesn't wholly extinguish those unhappy disagreements that are among Christians, it will at least so far lessen them that the fatal consequences of them will be prevented. (Henry, Matthew Henry's Commentary on the Whole Bible, p. 2303)

70

1 Thessalonians 5:11–14

In these words, the apostle exhorts the Thessalonians to several duties towards those who were nearly related to one another. They should comfort or exhort themselves and one another, and they should edify one another.

They must comfort (or exhort: the original word may be rendered both these ways) themselves and one another. And we may observe that those are most able and likely to comfort others who can comfort themselves, so the way to have comfort ourselves, or to administer comfort to others, is by compliance with the exhortation of the Word. Note, we should not only be concerned about our own comfort and welfare, but we must promote the comfort and welfare of others also. He was a Cain who said, "Am I my brother's keeper?" (Gen. 4:9). We must bear one another's burdens and so fulfil the law of Christ.

They must edify one another by "following after those things whereby one may edify another" (Rom. 14:19). As Christians are lively stones built up together into a spiritual house, they should endeavor to promote the good of the whole church by promoting the work of grace in one another. And it is the duty of every one of us to study that which leads to the edification of those with whom we converse, to please all men for their real profit. We should communicate our knowledge and experiences to one another. We should join in prayer and praise with one another. We should set a good example before one another. And it is especially the duty of those who live in the same vicinity and family to comfort and edify one another; this makes for the best neighborhood and is the best means to answer the purpose of society. Those who are closely related and have affection for one another, as they have the greatest opportunity, are under the greatest obligation to do this kindness to one another. This the Thessalonians did ("which also you do"), and this is what they are exhorted to continue and increase in doing. Note, those who do that which is good have need of further exhortations to encourage them to do good, to do more good, and to continue doing what they already do.

There is a mutual duty between ministers and people. If ministers are to labor among the people, then the people must know them. As the shepherd should know his flock, the sheep must know their shepherd. They must know his person, hear his voice, acknowledge him for their pastor, and pay due regard to his teaching, ruling, and admonitions. They must esteem their ministers highly in love; they should greatly value the office of the ministry, honor and love their ministers, and show their esteem and affection in all proper ways, doing this for their work's sake, because their business is to promote the honor of Christ and the welfare of men's souls. (Henry, Matthew Henry's Commentary on the Whole Bible, p. 2344)

71

Hebrews 5:2

Overlook not the ability of the Lord Jesus to meet all the infirmities of His people. There are two touching and expressive passages, in addition to our verse for today, bearing on this point. The first: "Himself took our infirmities, and bare our sicknesses" (Matt. 8:17). Wondrous view of the incarnate God! That very infirmity, Christian reader, which now bogs you down to the earth, by reason of which you can in no wise lift up yourself, your Savior bore. Is it sin? Is it sorrow? Is it sickness? Is it want? It bowed Him to the dust and brought the crimson drops to His brow. And is this no consolation? Does it not make your infirmity even pleasant to remember that Jesus once bore it and in sympathy bears it still? The other passage is this: "We have not an high priest which cannot be touched with the feeling of our infirmities" (Heb. 4:15). Touched with my infirmity! What a thought! I reveal my grief to my friend; I discern the emotions of his soul. I mark the trembling lip, the sympathizing look, the moistened eye—my friend is touched with my sorrow. But what is that sympathy—tender, soothing, grateful as it is—to the sympathy with which the great High Priest in heaven enters into my case, is moved with my grief, and is touched with the feeling of my infirmity?

Let us learn more tenderly to sympathize with the infirmities of our brethren. "We that are strong ought to bear the infirmities of the weak, and not to please ourselves" (Rom. 15:1). Oh, for more of this primitive Christianity! The infirmity of a Christian brother should by heartfelt sympathy become in a measure our own. We ought to bear it. The rule of our conduct towards him should be the rule of our conduct towards our own selves. Who would feel bound or disposed to travel from house to house, proclaiming with trumpet tongue, and with evident satisfaction, his own weaknesses, failings, and infirmities? To God we may confess them, but no divine precept requires their confession to man. We unveil them to His eye, and He kindly and graciously veils them from all human eyes. Let this be our attitude and conduct towards a weak and erring brother. Let us rather part with our right hand than publish his infirmity to others and thus wound the Head by an unkind and unholy exposure of the faults and frailties of a member of His body, and by so doing cause the enemies of Christ to blaspheme that worthy name by which we are called.

Honor and glorify the Spirit, who so graciously and kindly sympathizes with our infirmities. Pay to Him divine worship, yield to Him divine homage, and let your unreserved obedience to His commands, your jealous regard for His honor, and your faithful hearkening to the gentle accents of His "still, small voice" manifest how deeply sensible you are of His love, His grace, and His faithfulness in sympathizing with your sorrows, in supplying your need, and in making your burdens and infirmities all and entirely His own.

Nor let us forget that Jesus is so condescending that He regards Himself as honored by the confidence which places our sorrows upon His heart. The infirmity which we bring to His grace, the sin which we bring to His atonement, and the trials which we bring to His sympathy unfold Jesus as He is, and so He is glorified. Consequently, the more frequently we come, the more welcome we are, and the more precious does Jesus become. (Winslow, Evening Thoughts, February 14)

72

Matthew 20:25–28

How then shall it be among the disciples of Christ? Christ Himself had spoken of something of greatness among them, and here He explains it. "He that will be great among you, that will be chief, that would really be so and would be found to be so at last, let him be your minister, your servant."

Here observe that it is the duty of Christ's disciples to serve one another for mutual edification. This includes both humility and usefulness. The followers of Christ must be ready to stoop to the lowest offices of love for the good of one another, must submit to one another, edify one another, and please one another for good (1Peter 5:5; Eph. 5:21; Rom. 14:19; 15:2). The great apostle made himself every one's servant (1 Cor. 9:19).

It is the dignity of Christ's disciples to discharge this duty faithfully. The way to be great and chief is to be humble and serving. Who are to be best accounted of and most respected in the church, and will be so by all that understand things correctly? Not those who are dignified with high and mighty names, like the names of the great ones of the earth that appear in pomp and assume to themselves proportionate power. Rather, it is those that are most humble and self-denying and lay out themselves most to do good, though to the diminishing of themselves. These honor God most, and these He will honor. As he that would be wise must become a fool, so he that would be chief must become a servant. The apostle Paul was a great example of this: he labored more abundantly than they all, making himself (as some would call it) a drudge to his work. And is he not chief? Do we not by consent call him the *great* apostle, though he called himself less than the least? And perhaps our Lord Jesus had an eye to him when He said they were last that should be first. For Paul was "one born out of due time" (1 Cor. 15:8)—not only the youngest child of the family of the apostles but a posthumous one; yet he became greatest. And perhaps it was he for whom the first post of honor in Christ's kingdom was reserved and prepared by his Father—not for James, who sought it. Therefore, just before Paul began to be famous as an apostle, Providence so ordered it that James was cut off (Acts 12:2), that in the college of the twelve Paul might be substituted in his place. (Henry, Matthew Henry's Commentary on the Whole Bible, p. 1718)

73

John 1:16-17

The word "fullness" in this passage is sometimes used to express the idea of abundance. "The earth is the Lord's, and the fullness thereof" (Ps. 24:1); that is, the abundance of the earth is the Lord's. But in this connection, it has an even more impressive meaning. It signifies not only the fullness of abundance but the fullness of redundance. The vessel is not only full to the brim, but it runs over and rushes on in ten thousand streams to the utmost limit of man's necessities. Such a redundance of grace was required to bring God and the sinner together. The gulf which separated these two extremes of being was just that which separates the bottomless pit in hell from the highest throne in glory. No finite being could annihilate it. All the resources of wisdom, and power, and benevolence of all the angels in heaven could not bridge it. But the redundant grace that is in Christ Jesus has crossed this gulf, and God and man meet and are reconciled in one Mediator. And now, from the glorious heights of pardoning grace on which he stands, the sinner can look down upon a hell deserved but a hell escaped.

Such a redundant fullness of grace was never seen until Jesus appeared. The patriarchs and prophets saw this grace, but not as we are privileged to see it. They realized its sufficiency but not its redundancy. The truth was revealed to them, but by degrees. The light beamed in upon their minds, but in solitary rays. The grace distilled rather than flowed. They had the dew rather than the showers of grace. And yet it was sufficient to meet their need. When Jehovah opened this fountain of grace to two of the greatest sinners the world ever saw and declared that the seed of the woman should bruise the serpent's head (Gen. 3:15), dim and partial as was the discovery, it was sufficient to lift them from the dark borders of despair and hell, into the sunny region of hope and heaven. Thus, the saints of the former dispensation saw this grace, but not so clearly as we see it. They dwelt amid the shadows, we in the full blaze of glory. They lived in the twilight of grace, but we in its brightest day. They had the law, but we have the gospel. They had grace in the hands of Moses, but we have grace in the hands of Jesus. They were the children of the bondwoman, but we are the children of the free woman. They had the spirit of bondage unto fear, but we have the spirit of adoption unto love. And one passage will explain the reason of this great difference: "God, who at sundry times and in diverse manners spoke in time past unto the fathers by the prophets, has in these last days spoken unto us by His Son" (Heb. 1:1–2). Spoken unto us by His Son! Behold the fullness, the redundance, the sufficiency of this grace! "The law was given by Moses, but grace and truth came by Jesus Christ" (John 1:17).

Such, reader, is the fullness of Jesus, this divine vessel of grace. And now, if this grace was sufficient for God—sufficient to enable Him to extend mercy to the utmost, to the vilest sinners, and yet remain strictly just—then, I ask, is it not sufficient, my reader, for you? If God, on the basis of this grace, can come forward and extend His hand of reconciliation to you, may you not with the plea of this same grace advance and extend your hand of faith to God? If there is no difficulty or reluctance on the part of God, why should there be any on the part of man? And has God ever hesitated? Has He ever refused on the footing of Christ's merits to save the penitent sinner, who, having heard that the King of heaven is a merciful King, has cast himself upon that mercy, like the servants of Benhadad, with sackcloth upon their loins and ashes upon their head, humbly suing for life? Never! It is the delight of God, as it is His glory, to prove the power and the sufficiency of His grace in Christ Jesus, to save man to the uttermost extent of his guiltiness and woe. How overflowing with saving grace does the heart of God appear in these words: "Let the wicked forsake his way, and the unrighteous man his thoughts: and let him return unto the Lord, and he will have mercy upon him; and to our God, for he will abundantly pardon" (Isa. 55:7)! Oh, place your empty vessel beneath this overflowing fountain of grace! And remove it not until, in its measure, it becomes the "fullness of Him who fills all in all" (Eph. 1:23). (Winslow, Evening Thoughts, April 10)

74

Hebrews 10:19-23

O you of doubting and fearful heart, looking at the waves rolling at your feet and well near sinking beneath their swellings, exclaiming, "Will the Lord cast off forever? and will he be favorable no more? Is his mercy clean gone forever? Does his promise fail for evermore? Has God forgotten to be gracious? Has he in anger shut up his tender mercies" (Ps. 77:7-9)? Behold the glory of God's truth beaming in the face of Jesus Christ, and doubt no more. So long as Jesus lives—lives as your Advocate, as your High Priest, as your Representative in the court of heaven—all is yours which the covenant promises and which His mediation secures. "The promises of God are all yes and Amen in Christ Jesus" (2 Cor. 1:20). Never will He break His oath, or falsify His word, or alter the thing that has gone out of His mouth. "Heaven and earth shall pass away, but my word shall not pass away" (Matt. 24:35). God says it, and let faith believe it because He says it. So essential is it to your comfort that I would repeat the caution: in all your dealings with the divine promises, avoid a Jewish faith. Do not look so much at the grace of the promise or at the thing promised—precious as both are —as at God in the promise. The promise is the heart of your Father speaking; it is the faithfulness of your Father performing. Rest not, then, in the blessing promised but in the veracity of Him who promises it, and then shall your faith have confidence towards God. (Winslow, Morning Thoughts, May 27)

75

John 4:23–24

Here we see the blessed change itself. In gospel times, "the true worshippers shall worship the Father in spirit and in truth." As creatures, we worship the Father of *all*; as Christians, we worship the Father of *our Lord Jesus*. Now the change shall be in the nature of the worship. Christians shall worship God not in the ceremonial observances of the Mosaic institution but in spiritual ordinances, consisting less in bodily exercise and animated and invigorated more with divine power and energy. The way of worship which Christ has instituted is rational and intellectual, and it is refined from those external rites and ceremonies with which the Old Testament worship was both clouded and clogged. This is called true worship, in contrast to that which was by types and shadows. The legal services were "figures of the true" (Heb. 9:24). Those that revolt from Christianity to Judaism are said to begin in the spirit and end in the flesh (Gal. 3:3). Such was the difference between Old Testament and New Testament institutions. We see it in the temper and disposition of the worshippers—the true worshippers are good Christians, distinguished from hypocrites. All should (and they will) worship God in spirit and in truth. It is spoken of as their character and as their duty. Note, it is required of all who worship God that they worship Him in spirit and in truth. We must worship God in spirit (Phil. 3:3). We must depend upon God's Spirit for strength and assistance, laying our souls under His influences and operations. We must devote our own spirits to, and employ them in, the service of God (Rom. 1:9). We must worship Him with fixedness of thought and a flame of affection, with all that is within us. "Spirit" is sometimes used to describe the new nature, in opposition to the flesh, which is the corrupt nature. And so, to worship God with our spirits is to worship Him with our graces (Heb. 12:28) in truth; that is, in sincerity. God requires not only the inward part in our worship but also truth in the inward part (Ps. 51:6). We must mind the power more than the form, must aim at God's glory and not to be seen of men. "Draw near with a true heart" (Heb. 10:22). (Henry, Matthew Henry's Commentary on the Whole Bible, p. 1937)

76

Isaiah 40:26-31

As the prophet's commission opened, so the chapter is closed: in giving a special comfort to the Lord's people. It is impossible to conceive in the whole compass of language anything more gracious, more affectionate, or more kind than what is here said of the Lord's love for Israel. Every glorious perfection of Jehovah, and all His covenant relations, seems here to be brought forward to give confidence to His people in the security of His promises. It would be to take away from this blessed passage to attempt any comment upon it. Every word is so plain, so sweet, and so gracious that he who is taught of God cannot possibly mistake the meaning. The soul that is under the influences of the Holy Spirit must receive the comfort of it. And how very tender is the Lord's manner of reasoning with His people about the unreasonableness of their timidity! "Why sayest thou, O Jacob, and speakest, O Israel" (v. 27)? Reader, may the Lord give you and me grace to enjoy the full blessedness of what is said here. Thousands who are gone to glory have been, while on earth, refreshed by it, and thousands there are still to be supported by the same during their pilgrimage state here below. Oh, for the Lord, who gives the Scripture, to give to you and to me, by His Holy Spirit, the enjoyment of the Lord in His

Scripture! Then we shall rest in the support of a God all-sufficient and all-gracious in Christ, to rise above all the changeable circumstances of creatures in us and about us, until we come to lie down in the everlasting arms of our Lord in the kingdom which is above. (Hawker, Poor Man's Old Testament Commentary, vol. 5, pp. 395–396)

77

Hebrews 13:1-6

This chapter opens with some very engaging exhortations, arising out of the previous doctrines. And we read, first, of the brotherly love of members of Christ's body and brethren in the faith. For as the church in heaven and earth is one, so Christ's love for each one and their love for one another should be formed upon His standard. From the love of the brethren, the church is next directed to regard strangers; simply as strangers, and from the case of Abraham's entertaining the heavenly guests (Gen. 18:3), an inducement is made that the church should give kind reception to strangers under the hope that there may be some of God's dear children among them and, as such, well known to Him, though unknown to them (Gen. 19:1-3). After this precept comes another; namely, of tenderness to those in bonds—not merely prisoners in the body but also those experiencing bondage of the soul. And indeed, in the times in which the apostle lived, there were opportunities for the exercise of compassion to both. Then follows a very delightful observation on the marriage state. And as all marriages of honor and purity are types of Christ's marriage with His church, it is very blessed to hear the Holy Spirit thus continually approving of it. This paragraph closes arguing the weakness of excessive anxiety for the things of the body, when God by His covenant promise has made such ample provision for His redeemed in the engagement first given to Joshua, and in him to all the Lord's people (Josh. 1:5). I do not comment further on these different subjects, since they are in themselves so plain as to need no comment. (Hawker, Poor Man's New Testament Commentary, vol. 3, p. 309)

78

Colossians 2:1–3

What was it that the apostle desired for them? "That their hearts may be comforted, being knit together in love" (v. 2). It was their spiritual welfare about which he was concerned. He does not speak of their being healthy, and merry, and rich, and great, and prosperous; rather, he desires that their hearts may be comforted. Note that the prosperity of the soul is the best prosperity, and it is what we should be most concerned about for ourselves and others. We have here a description of soul prosperity. It consists in the abundance of comfort in our souls: "That their hearts might be comforted." The soul prospers when it is filled with joy and peace and when it has an inward satisfaction which all the troubles outside of it cannot disturb. It is able to joy in the Lord when all other comforts fail (Rom. 15:13; Hab. 3:17–18). (Henry, Matthew Henry's Commentary on the Whole Bible, p. 2332)

79

Mark 6:30-44

We see here the tender care Christ took for the disciples' rest after the fatigue they had. "He said unto them," perceiving them to be almost spent and out of breath, "'Come ye yourselves apart into a desert place, and rest awhile'" (v. 31). It would seem that John's disciples came to Christ with the mournful tidings of their master's death about the same time that His own disciples came to Him with the report of their activities among the people. Note, Christ takes notice of the frights of some of His disciples and the toils of others and provides suitable relief for both—rest for those who are tired and refuge for those who are terrified. With what kindness and compassion does Christ say to them, "Come, and rest!" Note, the most active servants of Christ cannot be always engaged in business but have bodies that require some relaxation, some breathing time. We shall not be able to serve God without ceasing, day and night, till we come to heaven, where they never rest from praising Him (Rev. 4:8). And the Lord is concerned for the body. He considers its frame and not only allows it time for rest but also makes our bodies desire rest. "Come, my people, enter thou into thy chambers" (Isa. 26:20). Return to your rest, He says. And those that work diligently and faithfully may cheerfully retire to rest. "The sleep of the laboring man is sweet" (Eccl. 5:12).

But observe, Christ calls them to come away from others, for if they had anybody with them, they would have something to say, or something to do, for their good. If they are to rest, they must be alone.

He invites them not to some pleasant country manor, where there were fine buildings and fine gardens, but into a deserted place, where the accommodations were very poor and which was a place created by nature only, not by art, for quietness and rest. But this was consistent with all the other circumstances He was in. No wonder that He who had nothing but a ship for His preaching place had only a desert for His resting place.

He calls them to rest only for a while. They must not expect to rest long but only long enough to get breath and then go to work again. There is no continuous rest for the people of God till they come to heaven.

The reason given for this need of rest is not so much because they had been in constant work but because they now were in a constant hurry. There was no order or schedule to their work; "there were many coming and going, and they had no leisure so much as to eat" (v. 31). If proper time is allotted and kept for everything, a great deal of work may be done with a great deal of ease, but if people are continually coming and going, and no rule or method is observed in dealing with them, a little work will not be done without a great deal of trouble.

They withdrew, accordingly, by ship, not crossing the water but making a coasting voyage to the desert of Bethsaida. Going by water was much less toilsome than going by land would have been. They went away privately, so that they might be by themselves. The most public persons cannot help but wish to be alone sometimes. (Henry, Matthew Henry's Commentary on the Whole Bible, p. 1790)

80

Romans 12:1–8

Why do we present ourselves to Christ except that we may serve Him? "Whose I am, and whom I serve" (Acts 27:23). To be religious is to serve God. How? We must make a business of it and not be slothful in that business. "Not slothful in business" (Rom. 12:11). There is the business of the world—that of our particular calling—in which we must not be slothful (1 Thess. 4:11). But this seems to refer to the business of serving the Lord, our Father's business (Luke 2:49).

All the saints make up one body in Christ, who is the head of the body and the common center of its unity. Believers do not live in the world as a confused disorderly heap but are organized and knit together, as they are united to one common head and are activated and animated by one common Spirit. Particular believers are members of this body. They are constituent parts, which makes them less than the whole, and in relation to the whole, they derive life and spirit from the head. Some members in the body are bigger and more useful than others, and each receives vitality from the head according to its proportion. If the little finger should receive as much nourishment as the leg, how improper and prejudicial that would be! We must remember that we are not the whole;

we think above what is appropriate if we think we are. We are only parts and members.

Each member has its place and duties for the good and benefit of the whole and of every other member. We are not only members of Christ, but we are also members of one another (v. 5). We stand in relation to one another; we are engaged to do all the good we can to one another and to act together for the common benefit of the body (see this illustrated more fully in 1 Cor. 12:14–31). Therefore, we must not be puffed up with pride over our own attainments, because whatever we have, as we received it, we received it not for ourselves but for the good of others. (Henry, Matthew Henry's Commentary on the Whole Bible, pp. 2226-2227)

81

Acts 20:32

See here what he commends them to the word of God's grace for: not so much for protection from their enemies or provision for their families as for the spiritual blessings which they most needed and ought most to value. They had received the gospel of the grace of God and were entrusted to preach it.

Now he recommends them to that gospel for their edification: "It is able (the Spirit of grace working with it and by it) to build you up, and you may depend upon this while you keep close to it and are deriving good from it daily. Though you are already furnished with good gifts, yet this is able to build you up; there is that in it with which you need to be better acquainted and more affected." Note that ministers, in preaching the word of grace, must aim at their own edification as well as at the edification of others. The most advanced Christians, while they are in this world, are capable of growing, and they will find the word of grace to have still more and more in it to contribute to their growth. It is still able to build them up.

He also commends this word of grace to them for their glorification: "It is able to give you an inheritance among all those who are sanctified." The word of God's grace gives it not only as it gives the knowledge of it (for life and immortality are brought to light by the gospel) but also as it gives the promise of it, the promise of a God that cannot lie and which promise is yea and amen in Christ. The Spirit of grace is given by the Word as the ordinary vehicle to be the seal of the promise and the deposit of the eternal life promised. Thus, it is the word of God's grace that gives us the inheritance (Acts 10:44–48; 2 Cor. 1:21–22). Note, heaven is an inheritance which gives an eternal right to all the heirs; it is an inheritance like that of the Israelites in Canaan, which was by promise and yet by lot but was sure to all the seed. This inheritance is entailed upon and secured to all those, and those only, who are sanctified. For as those cannot be welcome guests to the holy God, or the holy society above, that are unsanctified, so really heaven would be no heaven to them. But to all who are sanctified, who are born again, and on whom the image of God is renewed, it is as sure as almighty power and eternal truth can make it. Those, therefore, who would seek to own that inheritance must make it sure that they are among the sanctified, are joined to them and incorporated with them, and are partakers of the same image and nature. For we cannot expect to be among the glorified hereafter unless we are among the sanctified here. (Henry, Matthew Henry's Commentary on the Whole Bible, p. 2158)

82

1 Peter 1:3–5

To be aware of this amazing power in the soul is to be born again, to be raised from the grave of corruption, to live on earth a heavenly and resurrection life, to have the heart daily ascending in the sweet incense of love and prayer and praise to where its risen Treasure is. It possesses, too, a most comforting power. What other than this sustained the disciples in the early struggles of Christianity amid the storms of persecution, which otherwise would have swept them from the earth? They felt that their master was alive; they needed no external proof of the fact. They possessed in their souls God's witness. The truth authenticated itself. The three days of His entombment had been to them days of sadness, desertion, and gloom. Their sun had set in darkness and in blood, and with it every ray of hope had vanished. All they loved, or cared to live for, had descended to the grave. They then had no arm to strengthen them in their weakness, no bosom to sympathize with them in sorrow, no eye to which they could unveil each hidden thought and struggling emotion. But the resurrection of their Lord was the resurrection of all their buried joys. They now went to Him as to a living Savior, conscious of a power newly born within them—the power of their Lord's resurrection. "Then were the disciples glad when they saw the Lord" (John 20:20). But is this truth less enlivening and precious to us? Has it lost anything of its vitality to quicken or its power to soothe? Oh, no! Truth is eternal and immutable. Years impair not its strength; circumstances change not its character. The same truths which distilled as dew from the lips of Moses, which awoke the angelic lyre of David, which winged the heaven-soaring spirit of Isaiah, which inspired the manly eloquence of Paul, which floated in visions of sublimity before the eye of John, and which in all ages have fed, animated, and sanctified the people of God, guiding their counsels, soothing their sorrows, and animating their hopes, still are vital and potent in the checkered experiences of the saints, hastening to swell the cloud of witnesses to their divinity and their might. Of such is the doctrine of Christ's resurrection. Oh, what consolation flows to the church of God from the truth of a living Savior—a Savior alive to know and heal our sorrows, to inspire and sanctify our joys, to sympathize with and supply our need! Alive to every cloud that shades the mind, to every cross that disturbs the spirit, to every grief that saddens the heart, to every evil that threatens our safety or imperils our happiness! What power, too, do the promises of the gospel derive from this truth! When Jesus speaks by these promises, we feel that there is life and spirit in His word, for it is the spoken word of the living Savior. And when He invites us to Himself for rest, bids us look to His cross for peace, and asks us to deposit our burdens at His feet and drink the words that flow from His lips, we feel a living influence stealing over the soul, a filling of the Spirit and a soothing like that of which the trembling evangelist was conscious when the glorified Savior gently laid His right hand upon him and said, "Fear not: I am the first and last: I am he that lives, and was dead; and behold, I am alive for evermore, Amen; and have the keys of hell and of death" (Rev. 1:17–18). Is Jesus alive? Then whatever else dies, our life, with all its supports, consolations, and hopes, is secure in Him. "Because I live, you shall live also" (John 14:18–20). He is a living spring. Seasons vary, circumstances change, feelings fluctuate, friendships cool, friends die, but Christ is ever the same. Oh, the blessedness of dealing with a risen, living Redeemer! We take our needs to Him—they are instantly supplied. We take our sins to Him—they are immediately pardoned. We take our griefs to Him—they are in a moment assuaged. (Winslow, Morning Thoughts, November 26)

83

Psalm 43

David here makes application to God, by faith and prayer, as his judge, his strength, his guide, his joy, and his hope, with suitable affections and expressions.

As his guide, He is his faithful guide: "Lead me, bring me to thy holy hill" (v. 3). He prays that God, by His providence, would bring him back from his banishment and open a way for him again to freely enjoying of the privileges of God's sanctuary. His heart is upon the holy hill and the tabernacles, not upon his family comforts, his court privileges, or his diversions. He could bear the absence of these, but he is impatient to see God's tabernacles again; there is nothing so pleasing in his eyes as those. He would gladly be brought back there. For this reason, he prays, "Send out Your light and Your truth; let me have this as a fruit of Your favor, which is light, and the performance of Your promise, which is truth." We need nothing more to make us happy than the good that flows from God's favor and is included in His promise. That mercy, that truth, is enough; it is all. And when we see these in God's providences, we see ourselves under a very safe guiding hand. Those whom God leads, He leads to His holy hill and to His tabernacles. Those, therefore, who pretend to be led by the Spirit and yet turn their backs upon instituted ordinances certainly deceive themselves.

David also prays that God, by His grace, would bring him into communion with Himself and prepare him for the vision and reality of Himself in the other world. Some of the Jewish writers understand by the words "light" and "truth" here the Messiah, the Prince, and Elijah, His forerunner. These have come, they say, in answer to the prayers of the Old Testament. But we are still to pray for God's light and truth, the Spirit of light and truth who supplies the need of Christ's bodily presence, to lead us into the mystery of godliness and to guide us in the way to heaven. When God sends His light and truth into our hearts, these will guide us to the upper world in all our devotions as well as in all our aims and expectations. And if we conscientiously follow that light and that truth, they will certainly bring us to the holy hill above. (Henry, Matthew Henry's Commentary on the Whole Bible, pp. 804-805)

84

Proverbs 25:15

Two things are recommended to us here, in dealing with others, as likely means to gain our point. The first is patience: to bear a present disagreement without being put into a heat by it, to wait for an appropriate opportunity to offer our reasons, and to give people time to consider them. By this means, even a prince may be persuaded to do a thing which he seemed very opposed to—this is true all the more of a common person. That which is just and reasonable now will still be so later, and therefore we need not urge our position with force but can wait for a more convenient time.

The second recommendation is mildness, to speak without passion or provocation: "A soft tongue breaks the bone." It soothes the roughest tempers and overcomes those who are most sour. It is like lightning, which, they say, has sometimes broken the bone and yet not pierced the flesh. Gideon pacified the Ephraimites with a soft tongue and Abigail turned away David's wrath. Hard words, we say, break no bones, and therefore we should bear with them patiently. But it seems soft words do, and therefore we should, on all occasions, give them prudently. (Henry, Matthew Henry's Commentary on the Whole Bible, p. 1012)

85

Romans 12:9–11

P aul speaks here of a respectful love: "in honor preferring one another" (v. 10). Instead of contending for superiority, let us be eager to give to others the preeminence. The apostle explains this elsewhere as, "Let each esteem other better than themselves" (Phil. 2:3). And there is good reason for it, because if we know our own hearts, we know more evil in ourselves than we do in anyone else in the world. We should be eager to take notice of the gifts and graces and performances of our brethren and to value them accordingly. We should be more ready to praise another, and more pleased to hear another praised, than ourselves. Some read this phrase as "going before" or "leading one another in honor." We should be interested not in taking honor but in giving honor. Strive to see which of you shall be most ready to pay respect to those to whom it is due and to perform all Christian offices of love (which are all included in the word "honor") to your brethren, as there is opportunity. Let all your contention be about which of you shall be most humble and useful and condescending. The sense is the same in Titus 3:14. "Let them learn to go before in good works." For though we must prefer others (as our translation reads it, (v. 10) and consider others as more capable and deserving than ourselves, we must not make that an excuse for our lying around and doing nothing, nor should we, under a pretense of honoring others and their serviceableness and performances, indulge ourselves in ease and slothfulness. Therefore, he immediately adds, be not "slothful in business" (v. 11). (Henry, Matthew Henry's Commentary on the Whole Bible, p. 2228)

86

2 Corinthians 4:16–18

In what respects will it be a glory revealed in us? It will be the glory of perfect knowledge. "Now we see through a glass darkly; but then face to face: now I know in part; but then shall I know even as also I am known" (1 Cor. 13:12). Oh, what an orb of intellectual light each glorified mind will be! What capacity of understanding will it develop, what range of thought will it compass, what perfection of knowledge will it attain! How will all mysteries then be unraveled, and all problems then be solved, and all discrepancies then be reconciled! And every truth of God's revelation, every event of God's providence, every decision of God's government stands out more transparent and resplendent than ten thousand suns. Do you, in your present search for spiritual knowledge, deplore the darkness of your mind, the feebleness of your memory, the energy of your mental faculties impaired, dimmed, and exhausted? Oh, rejoice in hope of the glory that is to be revealed in you, when all your intellectual powers will be renewed as the eagle's strength—developed, sanctified, and perfected to a degree surpassing the mightiest angel in heaven. Then shall we know God, and Christ, and truth, and providence, and ourselves even as now we are known. It will also be a glory in us of perfect holiness. The kingdom within us will then be complete; the good work of grace will then be perfected. It will be the consummation of holiness, the perfection of purity. No more sin! The conscience no more sullied, the thoughts no more defiled, the affections no more ensnared, but a glory of holiness, dazzling and resplendent, beyond an angel's, revealed in us. "It does not yet appear what we shall be: but we know that when he shall appear, we shall be like him" (1 John 3:2).

The glory of perfect happiness will be the certain effect of perfect sanctity. The completeness of Christ is the completeness of moral purity. With reverence, we say that God Himself could not be a perfectly happy being if He were He not a perfectly holy being. The radiance of the glorified countenance of the saints will be the reflection of holy thoughts and holy feelings glowing within. Joy and peace and full satisfaction will beam in every feature, because every faculty and feeling and emotion of the soul will be in perfect unison with the will, and in perfect assimilation to the image, of God. Who can paint the happiness of that world from where everything is banished that could corrupt its purity, disturb its harmony, and ruffle its rest? That place where everything is included that agrees with its sanctity, harmonizes with its grandeur, and heightens its bliss? Oh, yes, it will be a glory revealed in us! The glory of the Father's adoption, the glory of Christ's atonement, and the glory of the Spirit's regeneration, radiating from a poor fallen son of Adam, a sinner redeemed, renewed, and saved. And what is each present ray of heavenly light, each thrill of divine love, each victory of indwelling grace, and each glimpse of the upper world except the foreshadowing of the glory yet to be revealed in us? Suffering and glory thus placed side by side, thus contrasted and weighed—to what conclusion does our apostle arrive? "I reckon that the sufferings of this present time are not worthy to be compared with the glory which shall be revealed in us" (Rom. 8:18). No, not worthy of a comparison. Do we measure their relative duration? Then, "our light affliction is but for a moment," while our glory is a "far more exceeding and eternal weight" (2 Cor. 4:17). Before long, all suffering and sorrow will forever have passed away—a thing of history and of memory only—while glory will deepen and expand as eternity rolls on its endless ages. Do we compare them? What comparison is there between the weight of the cross and the weight of the crown? Place in the scales the present "light affliction" and the future "exceeding and eternal weight of glory." Which is the lightest? Are they worthy to be compared? Oh, no! One second of glory will extinguish a lifetime of suffering. What were long years of toil, of sickness, of battle with poverty, persecution, and sorrow in every form, and closing even with a martyr's death, compared to one drink of the river of pleasure at Christ's right hand, one breath of paradise, one wave of heaven's glory, one embrace of Jesus, one sight of God? Oh, what are the pangs of present separation in comparison with the joy of future reunion? What are the deprivations of poverty now compared to the untold riches then? What of the suffering, and gloom, and contempt of the present time in comparison with the glory that is to be revealed in us? We can go no further. Tell us, you spirits of just men made perfect, if it is lawful, if it is possible, what is the glory that awaits us! Tell us what it is to be an unclothed spirit, to dwell in the bosom of Jesus, to see God, to be perfectly holy, to be supremely happy! Wait, my soul! Before long, it will all be revealed! (Winslow, Morning Thoughts, September 24)

87

Matthew 12:7-8

"God will have mercy and not sacrifice." Ceremonial duties must give way to moral ones, and the natural, royal law of love and self-preservation must take the place of ritual observances. This is quoted from Hosea 6:6. It was used before in vindication of mercy to the souls of men (Matt. 9:13). Here, it refers to mercy to their bodies. The rest of the Sabbath was ordained for man's good, in favor of the body (Deut. 5:14). Now, no law must be understood in such a way as to contradict its own purpose. "If you had known what this means," had known what it is to be of a merciful disposition, you would have been sorry that they were forced to do this to satisfy their hunger, and you "would not have condemned the guiltless." Note, first, that ignorance is the cause of our rash and uncharitable condemnations of our brethren. Second, it is not enough for us to know the Scriptures; we must also labor to know the meaning of them. Let him that reads understand. Third, ignorance of the meaning of the Scriptures is especially shameful in those who take it upon themselves to teach others. (Henry, Matthew Henry's Commentary on the Whole Bible, p. 1671)

88

1 Corinthians 13:12

The expansion and perfection of the intellectual faculties will result in a consequent enlargement and perfection of knowledge, and this is no inferior element of the future happiness of the redeemed. All that is gracious and sanctifying in the soul of the believer has its basis in a certain degree of spiritual knowledge. The mind is the medium through which the first communications of the Spirit are received. Knowledge of us has led to knowledge of Christ, and knowledge of Christ has laid the foundation of all the joy, peace, and hope the soul has experienced. As our spiritual knowledge increases—the mind becoming more and more informed in divine truth—there is a corresponding and proportionate increase of the blessing which an experiential acquaintance with the truth yields. Now, if this is so here, what must it be in the glorified state? Shouldn't we think that it will greatly augment the happiness and heighten the glory of the saints in heaven that in their enlarged mental capacity, in the fullest development of their intellectual powers, they shall be enabled to have a wider range of thought? That they shall possess a greater knowledge of God and see infinitely more of the glory and drink infinitely deeper of the love of Christ than the most exalted angel in heaven? If in the present school of God—often the school of deep trial—as we advance from truth to truth, knowing more of Jesus and increasing in the knowledge of God, we grow more holy and more happy, our peace flowing like a river and our righteousness as the waves of the sea, our confidence in God strengthening and our affections cleaving more closely to the Savior, what, we ask, will be the glory deepening around us when all the present obstructions and impediments to our advancement in spiritual knowledge are removed and our intellectual faculties, then unclouded and unfettered, expand their long-folded wings to sweep an infinite circle of intelligence—knowing even as we are known? If our progress in spiritual knowledge leads to an increase in our happiness here, what hereafter will be the felicity ever expanding our glorified souls through the medium of an enlarged mind—unlimited in its range of thought and pure and transparent as the atmosphere in which it exists? Do not consider it, then, you who are looking towards heaven, to be an inferior element of the glory that awaits you, that your intellectual enjoyment, perfect in its nature, shall ever be growing in its degree. "Then shall the righteous shine forth as the sun in the kingdom of their Father" (Matt. 13:43), and "then shall we know even as also we known" (1 Cor. 13:12). (Winslow, Evening Thoughts, June 7)

89

---

1 Corinthians 13:1-3

There is no truth more distinctly uttered or more emphatically stated than this, that love is infinitely superior to gifts. And in pondering their relative position and value, let it be remembered that the gifts which are here placed in competition with grace are the highest spiritual gifts. It is in this way that the apostle alludes to them: "God has set some in the church, first apostles, secondarily prophets, thirdly teachers, after that miracles, then gifts of healing" (1 Cor. 12:28). This is the way it is expressed here in the motto of our verses under consideration. We might phrase it, "Though I were an apostle, having apostolic gifts; though I were a prophet, possessed of prophetic gifts; or though I were an angel, clothed with angelic gifts, yet, destitute of the grace of love, my religion were but as an empty sound, worth nothing." Is there in all this any undervaluing of the spiritual gifts which the great exalted head of the church has bestowed upon His ministers? Far from it! The apostle speaks of spiritual gifts as excellent, but existing alone, they cannot bring the soul to heaven. And love may exist apart from gifts, but where love is found, even alone, there is that most excellent grace that will assuredly conduct its possessor to glory.

"Grace embellished with gifts is the more beautiful, but gifts without grace are only a richer spoil for Satan."

And why this superiority of the grace of love? Why is it so excellent, so great, and so distinguished? Because God's love in the soul is a part of God Himself, for "God is love" (1 John 4:8). It is like a drop of the essence of God falling into the heart of man. "He that dwells in love, dwells in God, and God in him" (v. 16). This grace of love is implanted in the soul at the time of regeneration. The new creature is the restoration of the soul to God, the expulsion from the heart of the principle of enmity, and the flowing back of its affections to their original center. "Every one that loves is born of God" (v. 7). Is it again asked why the love of His saints is so costly in God's eye? Because it is a small fraction of the infinite love which He bears towards them. Does God delight Himself in His love to His church? Has He set so high a value upon it as to give His own Son to die for it? Then wherever He meets with the smallest degree of that love, He must esteem it more lovely, more costly, and more rare than all the most splendid gifts that ever adorned the soul. "We love him because he first loved us" (v. 19).

Here, then, is that grace in the soul of man which more than all others restores to him the image of God. It comes from God, it raises the soul to God, and it makes the soul like God. How encouraging, then, to know the value which the Lord puts upon our poor offerings of love to Him! We may have no gifts, and even only a little love, yet of that little, who can fathom God's estimate of its preciousness! He looks upon it as a little picture of Himself. He sees in it a reflection—dim and imperfect indeed—of His own image. As He gazes upon it, He seems to say, "Your parts, my child, are humble, and your gifts are few; your knowledge is scanty, and your tongue is stammering; you cannot speak for Me, nor pray to Me in public, by reason of the littleness of your attainments and the greatness of your infirmity; but you do love Me, My child, and in that love, which I behold, I see My nature, I see My heart, I see My image, I see Myself. And that is more precious to Me than everything else." Most dear to Him also are all your labors of love, your obedience of love, your sacrifices of love, your offerings of love, and your sufferings of love. Yes, whatever blade or bud, flower or fruit, grows upon the stem of love, it is most lovely, and precious, and fragrant to God. (Winslow, Evening Thoughts, November 28)

90

Psalm 100

Pause, reader, pause my soul, and contemplate the numberless beauties and the vast sweetness contained in this short but comprehensive psalm. No wonder it is so often sung in our churches. No wonder, while it is sung, so many souls of true believers should feel such rich enjoyment in it, putting forth as it does the persons both of God and of His Christ, with the many rich blessings contained in the covenant relations of the Father, Son, and Holy Spirit. And shall not all lands, which are to see the glory of God in the face of Jesus Christ, join in the joyful noise? Shall not both Jew and Gentile, bond and free, rejoice together? Shall not, in every place, as the Lord has said, incense be offered unto Jehovah's name, with a pure offering, from the rising of the sun even to the going down of the same? Come, all you people, all you nations, both high and low, rich and poor, one with another! Come, sing forth the praises of Jehovah, the Creator, Redeemer, Sanctifier! Come into His presence with thanksgiving; enter His courts with praise. For He is indeed gracious, and He will receive the praise of His creatures in Jesus. Come, reader! Come my soul! Come, come before Him. He is justly entitled to our praise. He demands it; He expects it from us. Oh, for grace to worship Him in the beauty of holiness and to sing the jubilee song of salvation in and by Jesus Christ! Amen. (Hawker, Poor Man's Old Testament Commentary, vol. 4, p. 485)

Recommended Reading

Basics of Christianity

- "Our Triune God: Living in the love of the Three-In-One" by Philip Ryken & Michael LeFebvre (2011)
- "The Apostles' Creed: A Guide to the Ancient Catechism" by Ben Myers (2018)
- "Why Trust the Bible?" by Greg Gilbert (2015)

Introduction to Christianity

- "The Greatest Thing in the World" by Henry Drummond (c1880)
- "Maturity: Growing Up and Going On in the Christian Life" by Sinclair B. Ferguson (2019)
- "Now That I'm a Christian: What It Means to Follow Jesus" by C. Michael Patton (2014)
- "The New City Catechism" (newcitycatechism.com)
- "God's Big Picture: Tracing the Storyline of the Bible" by Vaughan Roberts (2002)

Works Cited

Hawker, R. (1808). *Poor Man's Old Testament Commentary: Deuteronomy-2 Samuel, vol. 2.* London.

Hawker, R. (1808). *Poor Man's Old Testament Commentary: Job-Psalms.* London.

Hawker, R. (1808). *Poor Man's Old Testament Commentary: Proverbs- Lamentations, vol. 5.* London.

Hawker, R. (1815). *Poor Man's New Testament Commentary: Acts-Ephesians, vol 2.* London: Sherwood, Neely and Jones.

Hawker, R. (1815). *Poor Man's New Testament Commentary: Matthew-John* (Vol. 1). London: Sherwood, Neely and Jones.

Hawker, R. (1815). *Poor Man's New Testament Commentary: Philippians- Revelation, vol 3.* London: Sherwood, Neely and Jones.

Hawker, R. (1845). *The Poor Man's Evening Portion* (A New Edition ed.). Philadelphia: Thomas Wardle.

Hawker, R. (1845). *The Poor Man's Morning Portion.* Pittsburg: Robert Carter.

Henry, M. (1994). *Matthew Henry's Commentary on the Whole Bible: Complete and Unabridged in One Volume.* Peabody: Hendrickson.

Spurgeon, C. H. (1896). *Morning and Evening: Daily readings.* London: Passmore & Alabaster.

Winslow, O. (1856). *Evening Thoughts.* Leamington, England. Winslow, O. (1856). *Morning Thoughts.* Leamington, England.

Robert Hawker (1753-1827):
Robert Hawker, a Royal Marine assistant surgeon, Anglican priest, and author, was born 1753 in Exeter, England. He was married aged 19 to Anna Rains, and they had eight children altogether. He was ordained as a minister in 1779. It was in the pulpit that "the Doctor" was best known and loved. Thousands flocked to hear the "Star of the West" preach when he was in London. An Evangelical, he preached the Bible and proclaimed the love of God. (Wikipedia: Robert Hawker 2020)

Matthew Henry (1662-1714):
Matthew Henry (18 October 1662 – 22 June 1714) was a British Nonconformist and Presbyterian minister and author who was born in Wales but spent much of his life in England. He is best known for the six-volume biblical commentary Exposition of the Old and New Testaments. (Wikipedia: Matthew Henry, 2025)

Charles H. Spurgeon (1834-1892):
Charles Haddon Spurgeon, an English Particular Baptist preacher and author, was born on 19 June 1834 in Kelvedon, Essex, England. He married Susannah Thompson in 1856 and had twin boys. Spurgeon remains highly influential among Christians of various denominations, among whom he is known as the "Prince of Preachers." (Wikipedia: Charles Spurgeon 2020)

Octavius Winslow (1808-1878):
Octavius Winslow, a pastor and author, was born on 1 August 1808 in Pentonville, a village near London. In 1834 he married Hannah Ann Ring and had ten children with her. He pastored churches in both America and England, spending most of his life in England. He was also known as "The Pilgrim's Companion," and was a prominent 19th-century evangelical preacher in England and America. (Wikipedia: Octavius Winslow 2020)